Physical Characteristics of the Standard Schnauzer

(from the American Kennel Club breed standard)

Topline: Should not be absolutely horizontal, but should have a slightly descending slope.

Back: Strong, firm, straight and short.

Tail: Set moderately high and carried erect. It is docked to not less than one inch nor more than two inches.

Hindquarters: Strongly muscled, in balance with the forequarters, never appearing higher than the shoulders. Thighs broad with well bent stifles. The legs, from the clearly defined hock joint to the feet, are short and perpendicular to the ground.

Coat: Tight, hard, wiry and as thick as possible, composed of a soft, close undercoat and a harsh outer coat which, when seen against the grain, stands up off the back, lying neither smooth nor flat.

Height: Ideal height at the highest point of the shoulder blades, 18.5 to 19.5 inches for males and 17.5 inches to 18.5 inches for females.

Color: Pepper and salt or pure black.

Feet: Small and compact, round with thick pads and strong black nails.

Standard
Schnauzer

◇

By Barbara M. Dille

9   **History of the** Standard Schnauzer

Read about the origins of the Standard Schnauzer breed, its evolution from German stock and its two popular offshoots, the Miniature and Giant Schnauzers. Meet early dogs and breeders and trace the Standard Schnauzer's path through the centuries and surviving the World Wars to become a recognized breed around the world.

17   **Characteristics of the** Standard Schnauzer

Learn about the breed's remarkable intelligence, versatility and trainability as well as its potential stubborn streak, propensity to bore easily, smartly furnished coat, unique sense of humor and potential health concerns. Find out if this medium-sized "big dog" is the right protector and companion for you and your family.

24   **Breed Standard for the** Standard Schnauzer

Learn the requirements of a well-bred Standard Schnauzer by studying the description of the breed set forth in the American Kennel Club standard. Both show dogs and pets must possess key characteristics as outlined in the breed standard.

30   **Your Puppy** Standard Schnauzer

Find out about how to locate a well-bred Standard Schnauzer puppy. Discover which questions to ask the breeder and what to expect when visiting the litter. Prepare for your puppy-accessory shopping spree. Also discussed are home safety, the first trip to the vet, socialization and solving basic puppy problems.

55   **Proper Care of Your** Standard Schnauzer

Cover the specifics of taking care of your Standard Schnauzer every day: feeding for the puppy, adult and senior dog; grooming, including coat care, ears, eyes, nails and bathing; and exercise needs for your dog. Also discussed are the essentials of dog identification.

74   **Training Your** Standard Schnauzer

Begin with the basics of training the puppy and adult dog. Learn the principles of house-training the Standard Schnauzer, including the use of crates and basic scent instincts. Get started by introducing the pup to his collar and leash and progress to the basic commands. Find out about obedience classes and training for other activities.

Healthcare of Your Standard Schnauzer **99**

By Lowell Ackerman DVM, DACVD
Become your dog's healthcare advocate and a well-educated canine keeper. Select a skilled and able veterinarian. Discuss pet insurance, vaccinations and infectious diseases, the neuter/spay decision and a sensible, effective plan for parasite control, including fleas, ticks and worms.

Your Senior Standard Schnauzer **128**

Know when to consider your Standard Schnauzer a senior and what special needs he will have. Learn to recognize the signs of aging in terms of physical and behavioral traits and what your vet can do to optimize your dog's golden years.

Showing Your Standard Schnauzer **134**

Step into the center ring and find out about the world of showing pure-bred dogs. Here's how to get started in AKC shows, how they are organized and what's required for your dog to become a champion. Explore some of the other competitive events in which the Standard Schnauzer participates: obedience, agility, tracking and herding.

Behavior of Your Standard Schnauzer **146**

Analyze the canine mind to understand what makes your Standard Schnauzer tick. Behavioral issues discussed include various types of aggression, separation anxiety, chewing, digging, barking and food-related problems.

KENNEL CLUB BOOKS® **STANDARD SCHNAUZER**
ISBN: 1-59378-324-8

Copyright © 2006, **2007** • Kennel Club Books® • A Division of BowTie, Inc.
40 Broad Street, Freehold, NJ 07728 USA
Cover Design Patented: US 6,435,559 B2 • Printed in South Korea

Library of Congress Cataloging-in-Publication Data

Dille, Barbara M.
Standard schnauzer : a comprehensive guide to owning and caring for your dog / Barbara Dille.
p. cm.
Includes bibliographical references (p.   ).
ISBN 1-59378-324-8 (alk. paper)
1. Schnauzers. I. Title.
SF429.S37D55 2007
636.73--dc22
2006011508

10 9 8 7 6 5 4 3 2

Photography by: Paulette Braun, Carolina Biological Supply, Bill and Catherine Dille Burdick, Lisa Croft-Elliott, Tara Darling, Isabelle Français, Jerry Glazman, Carol Ann Johnson, Bill Jonas, Dr. Dennis Kunkel, Joel Levinson Photography, MikRon Photography, Tam C. Nguyen, Photos by Susan and Lennah, Phototake, Jean Claude Revy, Joe Rinehart, Tien Tran Photography, Michael Trafford and Lionel Young Photography.

Illustrations by Gail Mackiernan and Patricia Peters.

Special thanks to Jerry Glazman and Arden Holst for contributing information about the breed in herding. Special thanks to Arden Holst for contributing the section on the breed's US history from the 1950s to the present.

The publisher wishes to thank all of the breeders and owners who cooperated with our photographers or submitted photos of their dogs for this book, including Constance Adel/Charisma, Diana Barber, Lucy Bitz, Bill and Catherine Dille Burdick, Cheryl Crompton/Stahlkreiger, Clive and Mary Davies, Rhonda Davis, Barbara Dille/Vortac, Linda Dobbie, Deborah Dunne, Douglas and Glenda Fisher, Ben Franzoso, Dean Gehnert, Gillian Goodacre, Grand Calvera Kennel, Sylvia Hammarstrom/Skansen, William Heidel, Arden and Earl Holst/Pepper Tree, Carol Karas, Linda Krukar, Judy Legan, Ron Lombardi/Bardwood, Anne S. Miller/Oakwood, Mary Moore, Boel Niklassou, Judy L. Rodrick, Hector Vigo, Lucille Warren/Von Stocker, Mrs. Jackie Watson and Barbara Weidner.

Artist and longtime breeder Gail Mackiernan captures
the essence of the Standard Schnauzer in her
drawings of a crop-eared pepper and salt and a
natural-eared black.

HISTORY OF THE
STANDARD SCHNAUZER

DEVELOPMENT OF THE BREED

There is no written record on how and exactly when the Standard Schnauzer was created. Over the years, knowledgeable dog people have discussed many theories. The most frequently heard theory is the one that is probably closest to the truth. This theory relates to tradesmen and farmers in 14th-century Germany who traveled the countryside and markets with carts laden with produce and other wares. The tradesmen needed a medium-sized dog of adequate size and strong enough to be a protection dog for their carts, but small enough to not take up too much space in the carts. These men, being of a practical nature, also desired that this new dog would be of service on the homefront as an excellent ratter, thus capable of double duty by keeping their stables and houses vermin-free. The breeders involved most likely crossed the black German Poodle and the gray Wolfspitz with Wirehaired Pinscher stock.

We do know for a fact that the Standard Schnauzer as we know it today appeared in several paintings by Albrecht Dürer (1471–1528), the most notable of which was his work titled *Madonna with Many Animals,* painted in 1492. Durer evidently must have owned a Standard Schnauzer, as later works of his contained seemingly the same dog as he aged.

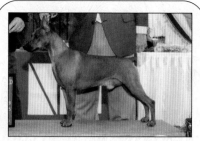

German Pinscher

A PINCH OF PINSCHER

In Germany, where the Standard Schnauzer was developed, the breed is grouped with the pinscher breeds in the German Pinscher-Schnauzer Klub (PSK). In the early years sometimes a breeder would have pups with smooth coats (pinschers) and pups with wire-haired coats (schnauzers) in the same litter. There are three sizes of schnauzer and three sizes of pinscher. The middle-sized pinscher (the German Pinscher, as it is known here in the United States) was near extinction after the two World Wars. Werner Jung, breed warden for the PSK in Germany, is credited with single-handedly saving the breed. The German Pinscher was introduced to the United States in 1982. In January of 2003 the AKC officially recognized the breed and classified it in the Working Group, where it joined the Standard and Giant Schnauzers. The German Pinscher's breed standard very closely resembles the breed standard for the Standard Schnauzer in all aspects other than the coat requirements. The German Pinscher has a short and smooth coat, colored in either solid red or black and tan.

A tapestry titled *The Crown of Thorns*, dated 1501, by Lucas Cranach the Elder (1472–1553), along with other works of his, also contained the likeness of a Standard Schnauzer. Rembrandt painted some Standard Schnauzers, and one appears in an 18th-century work by the English painter Sir Joshua Reynolds (1723–1792). This makes one wonder if the Standard Schnauzer was in fact in England during the 18th century or if Reynolds had admired the breed while traveling on the Continent.

We do know that the Standard Schnauzer, known as the *Mittelschnauzer* in Germany and simply as the Schnauzer in the UK and many other parts of the world, is the origin of the three breeds of schnauzer, the Miniature and Giant Schnauzers being the smaller and larger breeds, respectively. Many people are under the misconception that the Standard Schnauzer is just a larger or smaller version of his more popular cousins, the Miniature and Giant Schnauzers. The truth is that people were so impressed with the attributes of the original (*Mittel* or Standard) Schnauzer that other breeds were introduced into the bloodlines of the Standard Schnauzer to develop the Miniature and Giant Schnauzer breeds that we know today.

Although both the Miniature and the Giant bear a strong physical resemblance to our original Standard Schnauzer, the breeders actually created two distinctly different breeds. The family name "schnauzer" that all three breeds share probably derived in the early years of the Standard Schnauzer; this word refers to the dogs' distinctive appearance of having hair on their muzzles.

At the third International Dog Show in Hanover, Germany in 1879, Wirehaired Pinschers, as they were referred to then, were exhibited for the first time on record. Three dogs were entered from the Wurttenberg kennel, owned by C. Berger. The first-place winner was a dog named, fittingly enough, "Schnauzer." According to history, from then on all Wirehaired Pinschers were called "schnauzers."

In Germany, where the breed originated, the three sizes of schnauzer were put into the same club as the pinscher breeds, and they remain in that club today. In the US, the Standard Schnauzer is exhibited in the Working Group at dog shows along with his larger cousin, the Giant Schnauzer. In the UK, the Schnauzer is shown in the Utility Group along with his smaller cousin, the Miniature Schnauzer. In fact,

until the early 1990s, when the Giant was moved into the English Kennel Club's Working Group, all three breeds were shown in the Utility Group, which is similar to the American Kennel Club's Non-Sporting Group.

During World War I, the Germans used the Standard Schnauzer for Red Cross work as well as for dispatch work for the German Army. The desirable

ZWERGSCHNAUZER
The Miniature Schnauzer is known in its country of origin (Germany) as the *Zwergschnauzer*. This smallest of schnauzers shares the Standard's colors of solid black and pepper and salt, and additionally silver and black. In some countries, Miniatures are also seen in solid white. They stand 12 to 14 inches tall at the withers.

Miniature Schnauzer

RIESENSCHNAUZER
The Standard Schnauzer's larger cousin is known in Germany as the *Riesenschnauzer*. This is a very impressive dog with the same colors as the Standard Schnauzer. The Giant's height is 25.5 to 27.5 inches in dogs and 23.5 to 25.5 inches in bitches.

A comparison of the three schnauzer sizes, the Giant, Standard and Miniature.

breed characteristics of medium size, sturdiness and dependability made it a favorite of both the Red Cross and the Army.

Although there may have been an occasional Standard Schnauzer imported earlier into the UK, and records show that the first importation of the breed was around the year 1900, the first Standard Schnauzers imported in any great numbers into the UK were by the returning World War I soldiers who greatly admired these plucky and courageous dogs. The Standard Schnauzer preceded both the Miniature and Giant into the UK.

STANDARD SCHNAUZERS IN THE UNITED STATES
The Standard Schnauzer, often called by devoted fanciers "the dog with the human brain," is one of the most versatile breeds of dog. This becomes more apparent the more one lives, plays and works with this

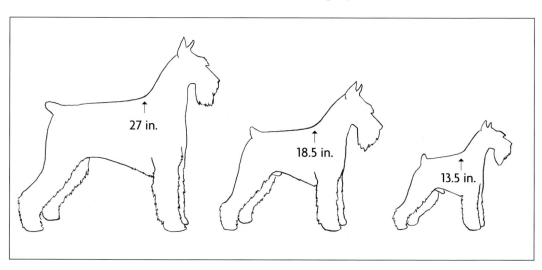

medium-sized, high-spirited breed. Standard Schnauzers are so versatile that even their classification for show purposes is often debated. We've mentioned that in England the breed is placed in the Utility Group, while in Germany it is found in the Working Group. Here in the US the breed is now rightfully classified in the AKC's Working Group, but this was not always so.

The cigarette case presented to first SSCA president, William D. Goff, by the AKC in 1934.

As in the UK, the Standard Schnauzer first appeared in the United States around 1900 and gained in popularity after World War I, when American soldiers began to bring them back home. In 1925 the Schnauzer Club of America (first called the Wirehaired Pinscher Club) was formed and included both the Miniature Schnauzer and the Standard Schnauzer, which were at that time classified by the AKC and shown together in the Terrier Group.

In 1933 the club divided into two separate breed clubs, but the two breeds were still shown together in the Terrier Group. The name of the original club was changed to the Standard Schnauzer Club of America (SSCA), with William D. Goff as the club's first president. In 1934 he received a sterling silver cigarette case from the AKC in commemoration of the first 50 years of the AKC. Since then, regional and local specialty clubs devoted to the breed have formed around the United States under the auspices of the national club.

For a glimpse of the breed in its early years of showing, let's look at the Northern Westchester Kennel Club show, which was held on Saturday, June 9, 1934 at Lawrence Farms in Mount Kisco, New York. In the Terrier Group, under the classification of Schnauzers (Miniature and Standard), there were three Standard class dogs and one

Ch. Pepper Tree Bel Air Rufnredy, "Nicki," shown with Laura Noll and owner Judy Legan, participates in the Standard Schnauzer Club of Southern California's first herding testing of the breed in 1998.

Standard champion bitch competing for the Best of Breed prize of five dollars. In the Miniature category, there were three class dogs, two champion dogs and three class bitches also competing for a Best of Breed prize of five dollars. That year both national breed clubs offered bronze statues of their respective breeds featuring the dogs who had accumulated the most points at designated shows throughout the year. The year was designated as starting with the Westminster Kennel Club show in 1934 up to the

Westminster show in 1935. It is interesting to note that the statue offered for the Standard Schnauzer was a bronze head study of Eng. Ch. Cranbourne Lupin. One wonders where that head study is now.

In 1945 the AKC's breed was moved from the Terrier Group to the Working Group, where it rightfully belongs and where it remains today, along with the Giant Schnauzer. The Miniature Schnauzer remained (and still remains) in the Terrier Group.

During the mid-20th century, as the US bounced back from World War II, the SSCA began to grow and develop into a broad-based national breed club. Officers were selected to represent all areas of the country. The national specialty show, traditionally held in the eastern half of the US, was now rotated annually from East to Midwest to West, allowing members throughout the country to participate. A regularly published national newsletter began in 1957 and the SSCA-published magazine, *Pepper 'N Salt,* originated in 1966. By the new millennium the SSCA had produced books, tapes and CDs and had developed a website.

The Standard Schnauzer has been predominately a family dog, home-raised, rather than kennel-raised, by a small core of devoted fanciers. This was

In Finland, the number-one dog all-breeds in 1983 and number-two all-breeds in 1984 was the American-bred Standard Schnauzer Swed./Fin. Ch. Skansen's Faenrik, owned by Mr. and Mrs. A. Nieminen.

especially true during the 1950s and '60s when even the top show dogs were family pets. Ch. Rick 'N Pat's Royal Rogue, SSCA Dog of the Year in 1959, 1960, 1962 and 1963, and Ch. Eric von Hahlweg, Dog of the Year in 1965, are prime examples, as both were groomed, trained and handled by their owners. In 1960 15 Standard Schnauzers finished their AKC championships, 9 individuals won a total of 17 Group placements and the most intensely campaigned dog, Ch. Stone Pine Storm, was shown 34 times. And so much more was to come!

As the club expanded and membership increased, interest and accomplishments in the show ring went through the roof. By 1990 104 Standards were shown to their championships and the top-winning dogs were shown multiple times every week. Now the top winners weren't just placing in Groups, but many were winning Bests in Show. Though a few were owner-handled, the majority was now groomed, conditioned and shown by professionals. Perhaps the most impressive overall record belongs to Ch. Parsifal di Casa Netzer, an Italian-bred dog imported by Barbara Dille for his breeder Gabriel del Torre, later owned by del Torre and Rita Holloway and shown by top

professional Douglas Holloway. He made history in 1997 by becoming the first Standard Schnauzer to win Best in Show at Westminster. During his show career, he was said to have accumulated 376 Bests of Breed, 157 Group Firsts, 130 other placements and 66 Bests in Show. In 1996 he was rated the number-one dog all-breeds in the United States. These accomplishments are impressive in any breed, and even more so in a breed that registers fewer than 600 dogs per year.

The show ring was not the only place of expanded Standard Schnauzer activity. The breed had always competed in obedience and tracking events.

Erik Basko van het Bakerveld, from the famous Dutch Bakerveld kennel of the 1960s, pictured weeks after winning a world championship.

Pictured here winning the Breed at Westminster, Am./Can. Ch. Oakwood Carolina Rebel, "Hilton," is a multiple Best-in-Show and national specialty winner.

An impressive winner of the new millennium is Am./Can. Ch. Charisma Jailhouse Rock, owned by Connie Adel.

"Standard Schnauzers Do It All," and the show included conformation, obedience, agility and herding.

The versatile Standard Schnauzer has been used as a therapy dog, search-and-rescue dog and police bomb-sniffing dog. OTCh. Tailgates George Von Pickel UDX, a Standard Schnauzer owned by retired policeman Duane Pickel, even served as a cancer-detection dog, detecting malignant melanoma with amazing accuracy. This is cutting-edge technology where once again this very versatile breed is proving to be a useful accomplice to man.

In the late 1980s agility hit the US and, as the new millennium arrived, AKC herding was added to the list of competitive activities for the breed. The theme of the 2004 national specialty was

The Standard Schnauzer has never experienced the same popularity with the general public as the Giant and Miniature; nonetheless, the future for this amazing breed should be very bright. The Standard Schnauzer will remain a loving family companion, and I suspect that most will continue to be home-raised by fanciers devoted to the breed. For all of the breed's accomplishments, the Standard Schnauzer is first and foremost a companion dog.

CHARACTERISTICS OF THE

STANDARD SCHNAUZER

The Standard Schnauzer is an exciting animal to see and to own. The clean, sharp beauty of this breed is impressive. The lively and individualistic personality of the Standard Schnauzer makes him a joy to live with. The Standard Schnauzer is truly one of the most versatile of all breeds. He is small enough for a petite woman to handle, yet large enough for even the manliest of men. He is robust and sturdy enough to be a working dog, yet small enough in stature so as not to be overwhelming. His ideal size, combined with the breed's properly maintained coat that has minimal shedding and little if any "doggy odor," lead many people to think that this is the dog for everyone.

However, nothing could be further from the truth. The breed's combination of intelligence and high spirit can make the Standard Schnauzer more than a handful for a lot of families. Remember, this is the dog that many fanciers refer to as "the dog with the human brain." Of course, the highly intelligent brain inside this sometimes very quick, active, agile body, when trained properly, does make the breed a very sensible and reliable working and companion dog—*proper training* being the key.

The Standard Schnauzer does not develop his full personality as a kennel dog. The Standard Schnauzer's mind develops best through close interactions with his human family. The breed in general has a very clever, inquisitive and sometimes creative bent. These dogs can also have mischievous and sometimes stubbornly determined minds. The Standard Schnauzer has a very strong sense of self-dignity, and the dog can be non-forgiving to people and children that have a propensity to tease dogs.

This is a true "people breed," and the Standard Schnauzer's brain needs the stimulation that only

With her distinguished looks and brains to match, the Standard Schnauzer will be an upstanding canine citizen with proper guidance from her owner.

The appeal of the Standard Schnauzer has led to its considerable fame around the world, celebrated on postage stamps and packaging for various products.

living with a family can provide. The Standard Schnauzer is not a one-man dog. Many will pick one family member as their favorite leader, but they readily accept all family members into their inner circle. Children must respect this breed's highly developed sense of dignity. They must treat their dog with respect; if they do, they in return will have an extremely loving, loyal pal. Only "real" family and a few select friends are ever privileged to the "wiggling from the inside out" tail-wagging welcome with which the Standard Schnauzer greets his special people upon their arrival home. This is a very selective greeting, one of the distinctive character traits of the breed. The Standard Schnauzer will learn to accept those close to his family, but this breed is protective over its home and family and needs to be properly introduced to new people by its family.

It is not wise to bedevil the Standard Schnauzer with needless tricks; he seems to need a reason for everything. Although he does have a good sense of "dog humor" at times, in reality he takes his job as guardian of the home very seriously. The family home and car belong to the Standard Schnauzer, and an unannounced visit brings out his deep bark, which from behind the closed door belies his medium size. He is exceptionally alert to his surroundings and aware of every change in them. His reaction is to

hold rather than to attack and, unless provoked, he has been known to keep an intruder cornered for quite a long time. Pity the letter carrier or delivery boy who does not take the time to make friends with this very big dog in a medium-sized package. His intense attitude at the backyard fence inspires respect from all who pass.

The Standard Schnauzer's coat is another feature that sets him apart

Taylor's instincts come to the fore as he detects "vermin" in the tree.

of soft downy-like hairs that should not be so profuse as to overwhelm the topcoat. The undercoat works like insulation, keeping the dog warm in winter and cool in summer. The outer coat offers excellent protection from the elements and easily can be brushed free of dirt.

There are only two acceptable coat colors: solid black and pepper and salt (or salt and pepper). This very distinctive coloration comes about because each of the guard, or outercoat, hairs is actually banded with color. Depending on the growth state in the hair shaft, it is either black or white. This is where the name for the coat derives: the dog looks like it has been sprinkled with salt and pepper. The texture of both the black and the pepper and salt colors should have the same harsh feeling.

Standard Schnauzers on the Continent today are often seen with undocked tails and natural drop ears.

from most other mid-sized breeds. He possesses a double coat that has a harsh coarse outer coat made up of stiff banded hairs that, when seen against the grain, stand slightly up off the back, lying neither smooth nor flat. The undercoat is composed

In the US, show dogs are almost always seen with ears cropped and tails docked the way they were back when cropping and docking were done for a reason—the reason being to prevent ears from being bitten by farm rats and to prevent tails from getting caught in wagon wheels. Even though the Standard Schnauzer breed standard does allow the dogs to be shown with natural ears and tails, it is indeed a brave and very knowledgeable judge who awards points to those dogs. Most show breeders and exhibitors prefer the cropped look as it makes for a sharper, crisper, more

The abundant facial furnishings are a defining trait of the breed's appealing look. This is a young dog from Pepper Tree Standard Schnauzers.

attention-getting dog. Many pet owners prefer the softer look of the uncropped ear. The ears in the UK and many parts of the Continent must be kept in their natural state, as ear cropping is forbidden by law. Even the tails in some countries on the Continent must remain undocked, due to new laws against tail docking. In the UK, if a breeder wants tails docked, a licensed veterinarian must do them.

Concerning health issues, which every owner must consider in determining if the Standard Schnauzer is right for him and vice versa, the breed is by and large a healthy, hardy one. It typically enjoys a long lifespan, upwards of 13 years and often up to 17 or 18 years. This is impressive for any breed of dog, no matter the size. Owners and potential owners should be cautioned, however, of some problems that have occurred in the breed over which breeders and vets voice some concern. Breeders worldwide are constantly trying to keep genetic defects to a minimum.

> **HEALTH TESTING**
> Reputable Standard Schnauzer breeders will have their breeding stock certified by the Orthopedic Foundation for Animals (OFA) as being clear of hip dysplasia, and will have current CERF (Canine Eye Registration Foundation) clearances on their dogs' eyes. Although eye disease is not prominent in the breed, annual testing is advised since eye problems can occur at any time in a dog's life and affected dogs should be removed from breeding programs.

Fortunately, however, Standard Schnauzers are relatively free of most of the genetic problems that can plague other breeds. Hip dysplasia (HD) has been documented in some Standard Schnauzers, though the problem is not as widespread as in most other working breeds, and severe dysplasia is rare. HD refers to the abnormal development of the hip in which the ball and socket fail to function properly. X-rays can determine whether the Standard

The three amigos: Taylor, Phlash and Stella enjoy some fresh air and sunshine.

HEART-HEALTHY

Most people obtain a dog for either companionship or show purposes. Research is now showing, through scientific study methods, that people who own dogs are also improving their health. For example, a study conducted at the UCLA Medical Center in Los Angeles involved a group of hospitalized heart-failure patients who would receive either visits from a volunteer with a dog, visits from just a volunteer or no visits at all. Scientists meticulously measured and recorded the patients' physiological responses before, during and after the visits. Their findings consistently showed the best results in the group of patients who received visits from a volunteer with a dog.

Think of what this means for pet owners. Studies have shown that petting, walking and grooming a dog all take positive steps toward lowering a person's blood pressure. Likewise, we all know that exercise is good for health and longevity, so your dog's daily walks will help you establish and maintain an exercise routine. It has also been found that senior citizens with dogs are not only more active but also less likely to experience depression than those without dogs.

Schnauzer is affected by this disease, which is considered to be inherited. Therefore, breeders routinely screen their stock so that dysplastic animals are not included in their breeding programs. Puppy buyers should discuss this with their breeders and ask to see documentation of the parents' hip clearances from an accredited organization like the Orthopedic Foundation for Animals (OFA). X-ray results are only conclusive once a dog has reached two years of age.

Very few breeders have encountered thyroid problems, eye problems or epilepsy, but there have been a few cases reported. Hypothyroidism refers to low activity of the thyroid gland; affected dogs require a thyroid-stimulating hormone (TSH) response test in addition to the standard t4 thyroid test to diagnose the disorder.

Snuggling with a canine companion is beneficial for both of you. Ch. Vortac Autumn Legacy CD is a registered therapy dog.

Epilepsy, in its inherited or idiopathic (of unknown cause) form, occurs in a number of breeds. It affects a dog's neurological system, resulting in recurring seizures or convulsions. Usually epilepsy can be identified when the dog is between six months and three years old.

The one problem that most frequently causes the Standard Schnauzer's early demise, besides the automobile, is one that is alarmingly prevalent in many breeds of dog (as well as in humans)—cancer. Discuss the prevalence of cancer in the breeder's line before committing to purchasing a puppy. Cancer can develop in an animal at any age, but it occurs most commonly at older ages. Breeders may have to research not just the grandsire and granddam of the litter, but perhaps go back as far as three or four generations.

Standard Schnauzers commonly suffer from minor skin problems; food allergies are fairly common as well, so owners must be aware of the chances of their dog's suffering from this nuisance of a problem. Food allergies are often treated successfully with dietary changes once the allergic ingredient has been identified.

Vortac Phantasia and Vortac Phantom Phly Boy may be active dogs but they still appreciate relaxation time with a friend.

Igor enjoys catching a wave on the beaches of his homeland, New Zealand.

STANDARD SCHNAUZER

Considered the "yardstick" by which the Standard Schnauzer is assessed by breeders and judges, the American Kennel Club standard for the Standard Schnauzer describes what is, indeed, the ideal representative of the breed. It is the standard to which dogs competing in dog shows are compared. The dog that most closely conforms to the standard, in the judge's opinion, is declared the winner (class winner, Best of Breed, etc). Breeders rely on the show ring as the proving ground of their programs. Only Standard Schnauzers who have been recognized in the show ring are thereby worthy of inclusion in a breeder's program.

There are many different standards for the Standard Schnauzer throughout the world, each kennel club adopting a different, though basically similar, standard for the breed. The American Kennel Club (AKC) and The Kennel Club of England each have their own standards, and the Fédération Cynologique Internationale (FCI) uses the German standard, from the Standard Schnauzer's native country. If you are planning on exhibiting your Standard Schnauzer outside the US, you must be aware of the differences between the standards from country to country. These will vary beyond ear cropping and tail docking to finer points of conformation.

It is wise to attend breed seminars and a few dog shows to help you better understand the American Kennel Club standard. Reading a standard is largely based on personal interpretation, as the standard is a somewhat vague guide to a very specific animal. Words like "medium," "strong" and "high" are relatively meaningless without being able to see actual quality specimens (so you can appreciate just how medium, strong and high a particular feature should be).

THE AKC STANDARD FOR THE STANDARD SCHNAUZER

General Appearance
The Standard Schnauzer is a robust, heavy-set dog, sturdily built with good muscle and plenty of bone; square-built in proportion of body length to height. His rugged build and dense harsh coat are accentuated by the hallmark of the breed, the arched eyebrows and the bristly mustache and whiskers. *Faults*—Any deviation that detracts

from the Standard Schnauzer's desired general appearance of a robust, active, square-built, wire-coated dog. Any deviation from the specifications in the standard is to be considered a fault and should be penalized in proportion to the extent of the deviation.

Size, Proportion, Substance
Ideal height at the highest point of the shoulder blades, 18.5 to 19.5 inches for males and 17.5 inches to 18.5 inches for females. Dogs measuring over or under these limits must be faulted in proportion to the extent of the deviation. Dogs measuring more than one half inch over or under these limits must be disqualified. The height at the highest point of the withers equals the length from breastbone to point of rump.

Head
Head strong, rectangular and elongated; narrowing slightly from the ears to the eyes and again to the tip of the nose. The total length of the head is about one half the length of the back measured from the withers to the set-on of the tail. The head matches the sex and substance of the dog. *Expression* alert, highly intelligent, spirited. *Eyes* medium size; dark brown; oval in shape and turned forward; neither round nor protruding. The brow is arched and wiry, but vision is not impaired nor eyes hidden by too long an eyebrow. *Ears* set high, evenly shaped with

moderate thickness of leather and carried erect when cropped. If uncropped, they are of medium size, V-shaped and mobile so that they break at skull level and are carried forward with the inner edge close to the cheek. *Faults*—Prick or hound ears.

Skull (Occiput to Stop) moderately broad between the ears with the width of the skull not exceeding two thirds the length of the skull. The skull must be flat; neither domed nor bumpy; skin unwrinkled. There is a slight stop which is accentuated by the wiry brows. *Muzzle* strong, and both parallel and equal in length to the topskull; it ends in a moderately blunt wedge with wiry whiskers accenting the rectangular shape of the head. The topline of the muzzle

Head study in profile showing correct structure, substance, type and proportion. The expression exhibits alert intelligence.

BETTER THAN THE AVERAGE DOG

Even though you may never show your dog, you should still read the breed standard. The breed standard tells you more than just physical specifications such as how tall your dog should be; it also describes how he should act, how he should move and what unique qualities make him the breed that he is. You are not investing money in a pure-bred dog so that you can own a dog that "sort of looks like" the breed you're purchasing. You want a typical, handsome representative of the breed, one that all of your friends and family and people you meet out in public will recognize as the breed you've so carefully selected and researched. If the parents of your prospective puppy bear little or no resemblance to the dog described in the breed standard, you should keep searching!

is parallel with the topline of the skull. Nose is large, black and full. The lips should be black, tight and not overlapping. *Cheeks*—Well developed chewing muscles, but not so much that "cheekiness" disturbs the rectangular head form.

Bite—A full complement of white teeth, with a strong, sound scissors bite. The canine teeth are strong and well developed with the upper incisors slightly overlapping and engaging the lower. The upper and lower jaws are powerful and neither overshot nor undershot. *Faults*—A level bite is considered undesirable but a lesser fault than an overshot or undershot mouth.

Neck, Topline, Body
Neck strong, of moderate thickness and length, elegantly arched and blending cleanly into the shoulders. The skin is tight, fitting closely to the dry throat with no wrinkles or dewlaps. The *topline* of the back should not be absolutely horizontal, but should have a slightly descending slope from the first vertebra of the withers to the faintly curved croup and set-on of the tail. Back strong, firm, straight and short. Loin well developed, with the distance from the last rib to the hips as short as possible.

Body compact, strong, short-coupled and substantial so as to permit great flexibility and agility. *Faults*—Too slender or shelly; too bulky or coarse.

Chest of medium width with well sprung ribs, and if it could be seen in cross section would be oval. The breastbone is plainly discernible. The brisket must descend at least to the elbows and ascend gradually to the rear with the belly moderately drawn up. *Fault*—Excessive tuck-up. Croup full and slightly rounded. *Tail* set moderately high and carried erect. It is docked to not less than one inch nor more than two inches. *Fault*—Squirrel tail.

Forequarters

Shoulders—The sloping shoulder blades are strongly muscled, yet flat and well laid back so that the rounded upper ends are in a nearly vertical line above the elbows. They slope well forward to the point where they join the upper arm, forming as nearly as possible a right angle when seen from the side. Such an angulation permits the maximum forward extension of the forelegs without binding or effort. *Forelegs* straight, vertical and without any curvature when seen from all sides; set moderately far apart; with heavy bone; elbows set close to the body and pointing directly to the rear. Dewclaws on the forelegs may be removed. *Feet* small and compact, round with thick pads and strong black nails. The toes are well closed and arched (cat's paws) and pointing straight ahead.

Hindquarters

Strongly muscled, in balance with the forequarters, never appearing higher than the shoulders. Thighs broad with well bent stifles. The second thigh, from knee to hock, is approximately parallel with an extension of the upper neck line. The legs, from the clearly defined hock joint to the feet, are short and perpendicular to the ground and, when viewed from the rear, are parallel to each other. Dewclaws, if any, on the hind legs are generally removed. Feet as in front.

EXAMPLES OF FAULTY BODIES

Head planes not parallel, i.e., down-faced, short thick neck, upright loaded shoulders, sloping topline and steep croup, which usually indicates rear quarters lacking strength and drive.

Generally lacking strength, substance and soundness; thin, ewe-necked, narrow front; upright shoulders; shallow chest; long back and soft topline; low tail set; lacking angulation behind.

Generally coarse, lacking agility and athleticism, short thick neck, heavy upright shoulders, coarse head and rounded topskull, thick heavy body, long-backed, low on leg, flat-footed, lacking angulation behind.

Very unsound and lacking strength and substance, head too long, severely ewe-necked, upright shoulders, shallow chest, very poor topline, high in the rear, low tail set, very weak rear, cowhocked.

Dog in profile, showing a mature specimen properly groomed. He is workmanlike and moderate in proportion and substance. He is strong, agile and athletic, showing pleasing type, sound construction and a dense salt and pepper coat.

Coat

Tight, hard, wiry and as thick as possible, composed of a soft, close undercoat and a harsh outer coat which, when seen against the grain, stands up off the back, lying neither smooth nor flat. The outer coat (body coat) is trimmed (by plucking) only to accent the body outline.

As coat texture is of the greatest importance, a dog may be considered in show coat with back hair measuring from $^3/_4$ to 2 inches in length. Coat on the ears, head, neck, chest, belly and under the tail may be closely trimmed to give the desired typical appearance of the breed. On the muzzle and over the eyes the coat lengthens to form the beard and eyebrows; the hair on the legs is longer than that on the body. These "furnishings" should be of harsh texture and should not be so profuse as to detract from the neat appearance or working capabilities of the dog. *Faults*—Soft, smooth, curly, wavy or shaggy; too long or too short; too sparse or lacking undercoat; excessive furnishings; lack of furnishings.

Color

Pepper and salt or pure black.

Pepper and Salt—The typical pepper and salt color of the topcoat results from the combination of black and white hairs, and white hairs banded with black. Acceptable are all shades of pepper and salt and dark iron gray to silver gray. Ideally, pepper and salt Standard Schnauzers have a gray undercoat, but a tan or fawn undercoat is not to be penalized. It is desirable to have a darker facial mask that harmonizes with the particular shade of coat color. Also, in pepper and salt dogs, the pepper and salt mixture may fade out to light gray or silver white in the eyebrows, whiskers, cheeks, under throat, across chest, under tail, leg furnishings, under body and inside legs.

Black—Ideally the black Standard Schnauzer should be a true rich color, free from any fading or discoloration or any admixture of gray or tan hairs. The undercoat should also be solid black. However, increased age or continued exposure to the sun may cause a certain amount of fading and burning. A small white smudge on the chest is not a fault. Loss of color as a result of scars from cuts and bites is not a fault.

Faults—Any colors other than specified, and any shadings or mixtures thereof in the topcoat such as rust, brown, red, yellow or tan; absence of peppering; spotting or striping; a black streak down the back; or a black saddle without typical salt and pepper coloring and gray hairs in the coat of a black; in blacks, any undercoat color other than black.

Gait

Sound, strong, quick, free, true and level gait with powerful, well angulated hindquarters that reach out and cover ground. The forelegs reach out in a stride balancing that of the hindquarters. At a trot, the back remains firm and level, without swaying, rolling or roaching. When viewed from the rear, the feet, though they may appear to travel close when trotting, must not cross or strike. Increased speed causes feet to converge toward the center line of gravity.

Faults—Crabbing or weaving; paddling, rolling, swaying; short, choppy, stiff, stilted rear action; front legs that throw out or in (east and west movers); hackney gait, crossing over or striking in front or rear.

Temperament

The Standard Schnauzer has highly developed senses, intelligence, aptitude for training, fearlessness, endurance and resistance against weather and illness. His nature combines high-spirited temperament with extreme reliability.

Faults—In weighing the seriousness of a fault, greatest consideration should be given to deviation from the desired alert, highly intelligent, spirited, reliable character of the Standard Schnauzer. Dogs that are shy or appear to be highly nervous should be seriously faulted and dismissed from the ring. Vicious dogs shall be disqualified.

Disqualifications

Males under 18 inches or over 20 inches in height. Females under 17 inches or over 19 inches in height. Vicious dogs.

Approved February 9, 1991
Effective March 27, 1991

STANDARD SCHNAUZER

WHERE TO BEGIN?

If you are convinced that the Standard Schnauzer is the ideal dog for you, it's time to learn about where to find a puppy and what to look for. The puppy selection process is not one that should be rushed, so be patient and do all your homework. You should inquire about established breeders who enjoy a good reputation in the breed. You are looking for a breeder with experience in dogs, outstanding dog ethics and a strong commitment to the breed.

New owners should have as many questions as they have doubts. An experienced Standard Schnauzer breeder is indeed the one to answer your many questions and make you comfortable with your choice of the Standard Schnauzer. An established breeder will sell you a puppy at a fair price if, and only if, the breeder determines that you are a suitable, worthy owner of his dogs. An established breeder can be relied upon for advice at any reasonable time. A reputable breeder will accept a puppy back should you decide that this is not the right dog for you.

When, as a prospective owner, you are looking for a pup, I suggest interviewing several breeders by telephone. You must be able to

A Pepper Tree puppy pile! The breeder uses colored string to identify the pups at this young age.

> **SIGNS OF A HEALTHY PUPPY**
> Healthy puppies are robust little fellows who are alert and active, sporting shiny coats and supple skin. They should not appear lethargic, bloated or pot-bellied, nor should they have flaky skin or runny or crusted eyes or noses. Their stools should be firm and well formed, with no evidence of blood or mucus.

relate to the breeder personally, as you will most likely be in contact with him often in the first year or two after bringing your pup home.

When choosing a breeder, reputation is much more important than convenience of location. Finding a local Standard Schnauzer breeder is out of the question in many areas of the US. If you do find a local breeder, you might find that that particular breeder is not planning to breed for quite some time. Many times a puppy-buyer will make arrangements to fly across the country to meet the breeder and bring back his newly purchased pup in an underseat pet carrier. Some breeders will ship their pups by air freight on direct flights. In this case, you would pick your puppy up from the major airport closest to you. You can contact the Standard Schnauzer Club of America (SSCA) at www.standard schnauzer.org for a copy of their breeder list; this is a list of SSCA member breeders who have agreed to abide by the club's code of ethics in their breeding programs.

Potential owners are encouraged to attend dog shows or competitive trials to see Standard Schnauzers in action, to meet the owners and handlers firsthand and to get an idea of what Standard Schnauzers look like outside a photographer's lens. Provided you approach the handlers when they are not busy with the dogs, most

NEW RELEASES

Standard Schnauzer breeders rarely release puppies until they are between 8 and 12 weeks of age; the actual age depends on whether or not the ears have been cropped and, if so, when. Usually a breeder will start the older pups on some sort of house-training routine that can be continued by the owners once the pups go to their new homes. Make sure that you take your new puppy to your own veterinarian, no matter what the pup's age, as soon as possible after bringing him home to ensure that he is a healthy pup.

are more than willing to answer questions, recommend breeders and give advice.

Once you have decided on a breeder who you like and trust, and whose dogs you like, do not be surprised if you are put on a waiting list. Sometimes it will be a year or more before you can obtain what both you and the breeder consider is the right puppy for you.

When it comes time to visit a litter, you must be familiar with the breed standard when looking at the dam of the puppies and at the puppies themselves. If the dam is a champion, your chances of getting a well-made puppy are increased. Whether picking a pup for pet or show, you want a healthy, sound, well-bred pup.

Picking a puppy is very difficult, even for the seasoned owner. I feel that usually the breeder, who observes the litter every day for the first weeks of the pups' lives, knows best which puppy will grow up to be the best dog for you and your family. This especially holds true for the breeder with many years of experience. Since Standard Schnauzers generally have large litters,

Even on-the-go Standard Schnauzer pups need to take a break sometimes.

> ## THE FAMILY TREE
> Your puppy's pedigree is his family tree. Just as a child may resemble his parents and grandparents, so too will a puppy reflect the qualities, good and bad, of his ancestors, especially those in the first two generations. Therefore it's important to know as much as possible about a puppy's immediate relatives. Reputable and experienced breeders should be able to explain the pedigree and why they chose to breed from the particular dogs they used.

averaging six to ten puppies, selection should be exciting once a desirable litter becomes available.

Always check the bite of your selected puppy to be sure that it is neither overshot nor undershot. This may not be too noticeable on a young puppy, but it will become more evident as the puppy gets older. Sometimes a bite that is slightly "off" will fix itself, while other times it will worsen. Discuss this with your breeder if you are concerned. Even if you are not going to show the dog, it is only naturally preferable to acquire a Standard Schnauzer who is properly constructed; a faulty bite could affect the dog's eating.

Breeders commonly allow visitors to see their litters by around the 5th or 6th week, and puppies leave for their new homes between the 8th and 12th week, depending on whether or not the ears have been cropped. Breeders who permit their puppies to leave earlier are more interested in your money than in their puppies' well-being. Puppies need to learn the rules of the pack from their dams, and most dams continue teaching the pups manners and dos and don'ts until around the eighth week. Breeders spend significant amounts of time with the Standard Schnauzer toddlers so that the pups are able to interact with the "other species," i.e., humans. Given the long history that dogs and humans have, bonding between the two species is natural but must be nurtured. A well-bred, well-socialized Standard Schnauzer pup wants nothing more than to be near you and please you.

A COMMITTED NEW OWNER

By now you should understand what makes the Standard Schnauzer a most unique and special dog, one that may fit nicely into your family and lifestyle. If you have researched breeders, you should be able to recognize a knowledgeable and responsible Standard Schnauzer breeder who cares not only about his pups but also about what kind of owner you will be. If you have completed the next step in this exciting journey, you have found a litter, or

GETTING ACQUAINTED

When visiting a litter, ask the breeder for suggestions on how best to interact with the puppies. If possible, get right into the middle of the pack and sit down with them. Observe which pups climb into your lap and which ones shy away. Toss a toy for them to chase and bring back to you. It's easy to fall in love with the first puppy who picks you, but keep your future objectives in mind before you make your final decision.

possibly two, of quality Standard Schnauzer pups.

A visit with the puppies and their breeder should be an education in itself. Breed research, breeder selection and puppy visitation are very important aspects of finding the puppy of your dreams. Beyond that, these things also lay the foundation for a successful future with your pup. Puppy personalities within each litter vary, from the shy and easygoing puppy to the one who is dominant and assertive, with most pups falling somewhere in between. By spending time with the puppies you will be able to recognize certain behaviors and what these behaviors indicate about each pup's temperament. Which type of pup will complement your family dynamics is best determined by observing the puppies in action within their "pack." Your

Puppies are adorable, but they are not ornamental. Make your decision to own a Standard Schnauzer with care and responsibility.

DOCUMENTATION

Two important documents that you will get from the breeder are the pup's pedigree and AKC registration papers. The breeder should register the litter with the AKC and it is necessary for you to have the correct paperwork if you have any thoughts of showing or breeding in the future. There are two types of registration, a limited registration and a full registration. The limited registration prohibits you from registering any future offspring of the dog and from showing the dog in the conformation ring but does allow you to enter your dog in obedience trials, agility trials and other working competitions. It is possible for a pup with a limited registration to be granted full registration status once he has reached one year of age; only the breeder can decide to change the registration, thereby allowing the dog to be shown and/or bred. Some breeders individually register each pup, ensuring that each pup carries on the kennel name. A booklet on registration policies can be obtained free of charge by contacting the AKC; send an email to info@akc.org.

breeder's expertise and recommendations are also very valuable. Although you may fall in love with a bold and brassy male, the breeder may suggest that another pup would be best for you. The breeder's experience in rearing Standard Schnauzer pups and matching their temperaments with appropriate humans offers the best assurance that your pup will meet your needs and expectations. The type of puppy that you select is just as important as your decision that the Standard Schnauzer is the breed for you.

The decision to live with a Standard Schnauzer is a serious commitment and not one to be taken lightly. This puppy is a living sentient being that will be

A young herder-in-training and his unsuspecting practice subjects.

DOG OR BITCH?

Male Schnauzers can be dog-aggressive. Most males will not deliberately start a fight, but they are always willing to finish it. A sexually active male is more prone to defend whatever he imagines as his territory. If there are no females living with them, two or more males can be raised together. If you plan to have two or more males living together, neutering all of them is highly recommended unless they are being shown or used as breeding stock.

Females on the whole are not dog-aggressive to their own kind, except during the first few weeks of raising puppies. Some females will "not so politely" tell a strange male to keep his distance. When males and females are housed together, in many cases the female is the dominant leader of the dog pack. It is most important to find the pup with the personality and temperament that meet your ideal, be it male or female.

dependent on you for basic survival for his entire life. Beyond the basics of survival—food, water, shelter and protection—he needs much, much more. The new pup needs love, nurturing and a proper canine education to mold him into a responsible, well-behaved canine citizen. Your Standard Schnauzer's health and good manners will need consistent monitoring and regular "tune-ups," so your job as a responsible dog owner will be ongoing throughout every stage of his life. Your new Standard Schnauzer puppy represents a longtime commitment that could last 15 or more years. Are you prepared?

Although the responsibilities of owning a dog may at times tax your patience, the joy of living with your Standard Schnauzer far outweighs the workload, and a well-mannered adult dog is worth your time and effort. Before your very eyes, your new charge will grow up to be your most loyal friend, devoted to you unconditionally.

YOUR STANDARD SCHNAUZER SHOPPING LIST

Just as expectant parents prepare a nursery for their baby, so should you ready your home for the arrival of your Standard Schnauzer pup. If you have the necessary puppy supplies purchased and in place before he comes home, it will ease the puppy's transition from the warmth and familiarity of his mom and littermates to the brand-new environment of his new home and human family. You will be too busy to stock up and prepare your house after your pup comes home, that's for sure! Imagine how a pup must feel

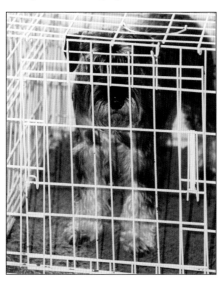

Your dog will view his crate as a place of refuge, not a place of confinement, if you introduce him to it correctly.

upon being transported to a strange new place. It's up to you to comfort him and to let your little pup know that he is going to be happy with you.

FOOD AND WATER BOWLS

Your puppy will need separate bowls for his food and water. Stainless steel bowls are generally preferred over plastic bowls since they sterilize better and pups are less inclined to chew on the metal. Ceramic bowls are popular, but consider how often you will have to pick up those heavy bowls. Buy adult-sized bowls, as your puppy will grow into them before you know it.

THE DOG CRATE

If you think that crates are tools of punishment and confinement for when a dog has misbehaved, think again. Most breeders and almost all trainers recommend a crate as the preferred house-training aid as well as for all-around puppy training and safety. Because dogs are natural den creatures that prefer cave-like environments, the benefits of crate use are many. The crate provides the puppy with his very own "safe house," a cozy place to sleep, take a break or seek comfort with a favorite toy; a travel aid to house your dog when on the road, at motels or at the vet's office; a training aid to help teach your puppy proper toileting habits; and a place of solitude when non-dog people happen to drop by and don't want a lively puppy—or even a well-behaved adult dog—saying hello or begging for attention.

Crates come in several types, although the wire crate and the fiberglass airline-type crate are the most popular. Both are safe and your puppy will adjust to either one, so the choice is up to you. The wire crates offer better visibility for the pup as well as better ventilation. Many of the wire crates easily collapse into suitcase-size carriers. The fiberglass crates, similar to those used by the airlines for animal transport, are sturdier and more den-like. However, the fiberglass crates do not fold down and are less ventilated than wire crates; this can be problematic in hot weather. Some of the newer crates are made of heavy plastic mesh; they are very lightweight and fold up into slim-line suitcases.

However, a mesh crate might not be suitable for a pup with manic chewing habits.

Don't bother with a puppy-sized crate. Although your Standard Schnauzer will be a wee fellow when you bring him home, he will grow up in the blink of an eye and your puppy crate will be useless. Purchase a crate that will accommodate an adult Standard Schnauzer. He will stand about 17.5–19.5 inches at the shoulder when full grown, and a proper-sized crate will allow him to stand up, lie down and turn around fully. Partitioning the crate into a smaller area is recommended for puppy house-training; Standard Schnauzers learn proper toileting through crate-training quickly when compared to some other breeds.

Vortac Absolute Phlashback, "Phlash," as a youngster with his ears bridged as part of ear-cropping aftercare.

Bedding doesn't have to be fancy to be comfortable for a puppy.

BEDDING AND CRATE PADS

Your puppy will enjoy some type of soft bedding in his "room" (the crate), something he can snuggle into to feel cozy and secure. Old towels or blankets are good choices for a young pup, since he may (and probably will) have a toileting accident or two in the crate or decide to chew on the bedding material. Once he is fully trained and out of the early chewing stage, you can replace the puppy bedding with a permanent crate pad if you prefer. Crate pads and other dog beds run the gamut from inexpensive to high-end doggie-designer styles, but don't splurge on the good stuff until you are sure that your puppy is reliable and won't tear it up or make a mess on it.

PUPPY TOYS

Just as infants and older children require objects to stimulate their minds and bodies, puppies need toys to entertain their curious brains, wiggly paws and achy teeth. A fun array of safe doggie toys will help satisfy your puppy's chewing instincts and distract him from gnawing on the leg of your antique chair or your new leather sofa. Most puppy toys are cute and look as if they would be a lot of fun, but not all are necessarily safe or good for your puppy, so use caution when you go puppy-toy shopping.

Most Standard Schnauzers are chewers, not only during puppyhood but also throughout their adult lives. Luckily, they can be taught to chew only on appropriate dog toys. The Standard Schnauzer is a very intelligent dog and consequently gets bored easily. Try using a toy box filled with many different shapes, textures and sizes of toys. Stuffed plush animals are very much favored, and most Standard Schnauzers delight in "de-stuffing" them, but will continue to play with them even after the stuffing is all out. These unstuffed wet plush carcasses are usually the ones picked up by Standard Schnauzers when greeting guests at the door. Be careful that the dog doesn't eat the "innards" of these toys, as this can be dangerous.

Soft natural latex squeak toys are also favorites, but these too must be carefully monitored so that they are not torn apart and the squeakers eaten. Hard toys

Standard Schnauzers should stay happily occupied if given an array of safe and interesting toys to chew.

such as natural shank bones, nylon bones, hard rubber toys and pigs' feet or cow hooves are also excellent boredom chasers. Be very vigilant, though, in removing them when they break into pieces or become small enough for the Standard Schnauzer to swallow whole. Standard Schnauzers have been known to swallow small items when confronted with the prospect of losing the item to their owners or to other dogs.

Rawhide bones are not recommended, as they are too easily eaten and qualify as empty calories, leading to overweight dogs. Plus, they can damage the leg and facial furnishings as well as cause intestinal blockages or choking.

If you believe that your pup has ingested a piece of one of his toys, check his stools for the next couple of days to see if he passes the item when he defecates. At the same time, also watch for signs of intestinal distress. A call to your veterinarian might be in order to get his advice and be on the safe side.

An all-time favorite toy for puppies (young and old!) is the empty gallon milk jug. Hard plastic juice containers—46 ounces or more—are also excellent. Such containers make lots of noise when they are batted about, and puppies go crazy with delight as they play with them. However, they don't

often last very long, so be sure to remove and replace them when they get chewed up.

A word of caution about homemade toys: be careful with your choices of non-traditional play objects. Never use old shoes or socks, since a puppy cannot distinguish between the old ones on which he's allowed to chew and the new ones in your closet that are strictly off limits. That principle applies to anything that resembles something that you don't want your puppy to chew.

COLLARS

A lightweight nylon collar is the best choice for a very young pup. Quick-click collars are easy to put on and remove, and they can be adjusted as the puppy grows. Introduce him to his collar as soon as he comes home to get him accustomed to wearing it. He'll get used to it quickly and won't mind a bit. Make sure that it is snug enough that it won't slip off, yet loose enough to be comfortable for the pup. You

Finding something soft to sink his teeth into is a priority of every pup, especially while teething.

should be able to slip two fingers between the collar and his neck. Check the collar for proper fit at least once a week, as the young pup grows rapidly and soon outgrows his collar. Most pups go through three or four collar sizes before reaching their adult size. There are many other types of collars and head halters, but these should only be used under an expert's watchful eye and will not be needed for a young puppy.

LEASHES

A 6-foot lead is an excellent choice for a young puppy. Leather leashes are the most comfortable

Ch. Ahrenfeld Destiny von Vortac CD is ready for a walk...can you tell?

in the hand and are the type that trainers prefer. For initial puppy walks and house-training purposes, you should invest in a shorter lead so that you have more control over the puppy. At first, you don't want him wandering too far away from you, and when taking him out for toileting you will want to keep him in the specific area chosen for his potty spot.

Resist the temptation to use a retractable leash until the puppy respects you as the leader of his walks. Used earlier than this, the retractable leash tells the puppy that he can go wherever his nose takes him and you will follow— not a good idea!

HOME SAFETY FOR YOUR PUPPY

The importance of puppy-proofing cannot be overstated. In addition to making your house comfortable for your Standard Schnauzer's arrival, you also must make sure that your house is safe for your puppy before you bring him home. There are countless hazards in the owner's personal living environment that a pup can sniff, chew, swallow or destroy. Many are obvious; others are not. Do a thorough advance house check to remove or rearrange those things that could hurt your puppy, keeping any potentially dangerous items out of areas to which he will have access.

Collaring Our Canines

The standard flat collar with a buckle or a snap, in leather, nylon or cotton, is widely regarded as the everyday all-purpose collar. If the collar fits correctly, you should be able to fit two fingers between the collar and the dog's neck.

Leather Buckle Collars

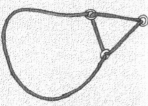

Limited-Slip Collar

The martingale, Greyhound or limited-slip collar is preferred by many dog owners and trainers. It is fixed with an extra loop that tightens when pressure is applied to the leash. The martingale collar gets tighter but does not "choke" the dog. The limited-slip collar should only be used for walking and training, not for free play or interaction with another dog. These types of collar should never be left on the dog, as the extra loop can lead to accidents.

Choke collars, usually made of stainless steel, are made for training purposes but are not recommended for small dogs or heavily coated breeds. The chains can injure small dogs or damage long/abundant coats. Thin nylon choke leads are commonly used on show dogs while in the ring, though they are not practical for everyday use.

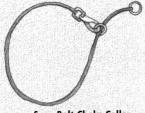

Snap-Bolt Choke Collar

The harness, with two or three straps that attach over the dog's shoulders and around his torso, is a humane and safe alternative to the

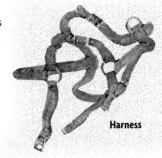

Harness

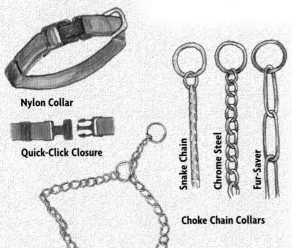

Nylon Collar

Quick-Click Closure

Snake Chain

Chrome Steel

Fur-Saver

Choke Chain Collars

conventional collar. By and large, a well-made harness is virtually escape-proof. Harnesses are available in nylon and mesh and can be outfitted on most dogs with chest girths ranging from 10 to 30 inches.

A head collar, composed of a nylon strap that goes around the dog's muzzle and a second strap that wraps around his neck, offers the owner better control over his dog. This device is recommended for problem-solving with dogs (including jumping up, pulling and aggressive behaviors) but must be used with care.

A Dog-Safe Home

The dog-safety police are taking you on a house tour. Let's go room by room and see how safe your own home is for your Standard Schnauzer. The following items are doggie dangers, so either they must be removed or the dog should be monitored or not allowed access to these areas.

Living Room

- house plants (some varieties are poisonous)
- fireplace or wood-burning stove
- paint on the walls (lead-based paint is toxic)
- lead drapery weights (toxic lead)
- lamps and electrical cords
- carpet cleaners or deodorizers

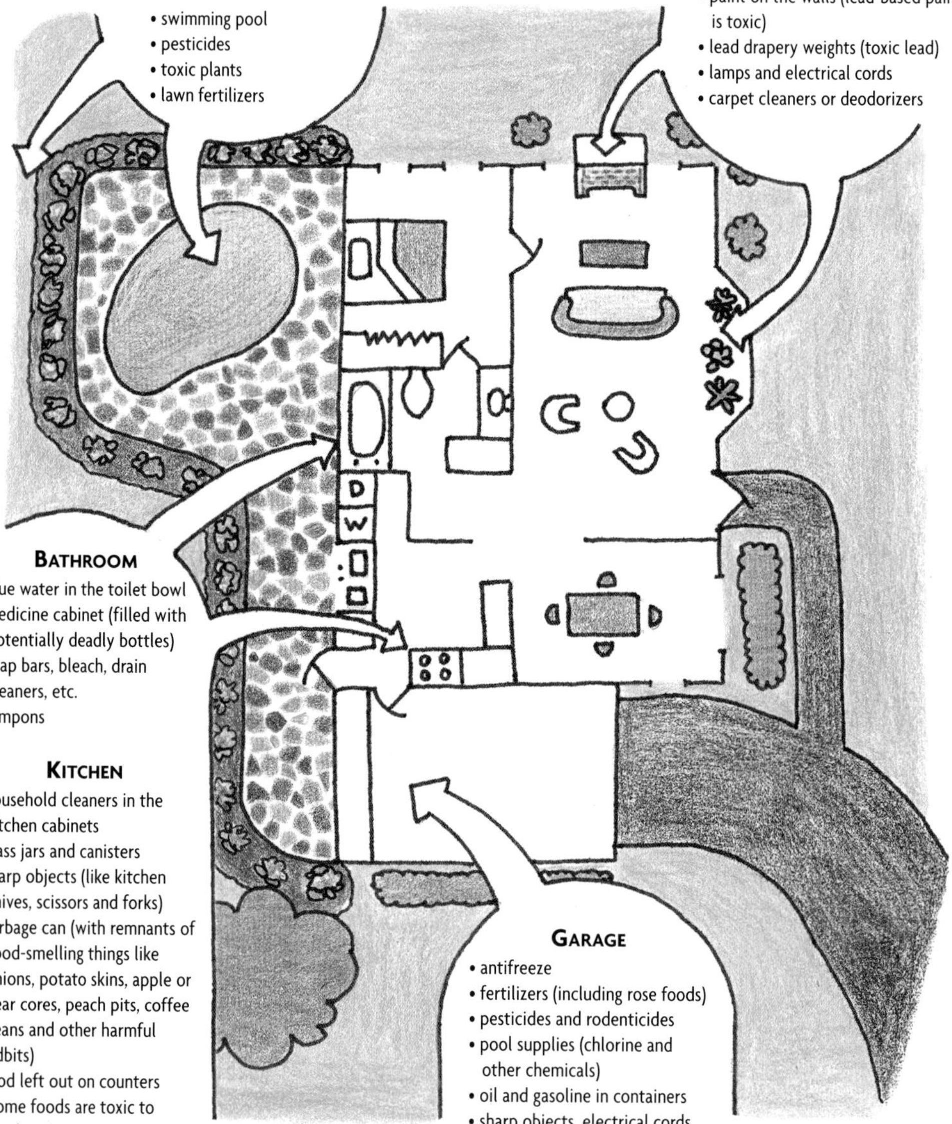

Outdoors

- swimming pool
- pesticides
- toxic plants
- lawn fertilizers

Bathroom

- blue water in the toilet bowl
- medicine cabinet (filled with potentially deadly bottles)
- soap bars, bleach, drain cleaners, etc.
- tampons

Kitchen

- household cleaners in the kitchen cabinets
- glass jars and canisters
- sharp objects (like kitchen knives, scissors and forks)
- garbage can (with remnants of good-smelling things like onions, potato skins, apple or pear cores, peach pits, coffee beans and other harmful tidbits)
- food left out on counters (some foods are toxic to dogs)

Garage

- antifreeze
- fertilizers (including rose foods)
- pesticides and rodenticides
- pool supplies (chlorine and other chemicals)
- oil and gasoline in containers
- sharp objects, electrical cords and power tools

Electrical cords are especially dangerous, since puppies view them as irresistible chew toys. Unplug and remove all exposed cords or fasten them beneath baseboards where the puppy cannot reach them. Veterinarians and firefighters can tell you horror stories about electrical burns and house fires that resulted from puppy-chewed electrical cords. Consider this a most serious precaution for your puppy and the rest of your family.

Scout your home for tiny objects that might be seen at a pup's eye level. Keep medication bottles and cleaning supplies well out of reach, and do the same with waste baskets and other trash containers. It goes without saying that you should not use rodent poison or other toxic chemicals in any puppy area and that you must keep such containers safely locked up. You will be amazed at how many places a curious puppy can discover!

Once your house has cleared inspection, check your yard. Most Standard Schnauzers are not climbers, but they are excellent jumpers and diggers. A 6-foot-high fence with an additional 10–12 inches buried below the surface is usually sufficient to contain a Standard Schnauzer, although some very motivated Standard Schnauzers have scaled fences of this height. Check the fence periodically for necessary repairs. If there is a weak link or space to squeeze through, you can be sure that a determined Standard Schnauzer will discover it.

Many owners fence off their flower beds separately, as sometimes the Standard Schnauzer likes to do some "gardening." I know of one breeder who keeps all flowers in pots raised at least 18 inches so that they are not inadvertently "watered" by the males.

The garage and shed can be hazardous places for a pup, as things like fertilizers, chemicals

When it comes to an enticing aroma, Standard Schnauzers are more than merely inquisitive; they can be downright nosy.

For some reason, grass is a favorite snack of many pups—all the more reason to make sure that your lawn is chemical-free and be careful about where your dog grazes.

and tools are usually kept there. It's best to keep these areas off limits to the pup. Antifreeze is especially dangerous to dogs, as they find the taste appealing and it takes only a few licks from the driveway to kill a dog, puppy or adult, small breed or large.

VISITING THE VETERINARIAN

A good veterinarian is your Standard Schnauzer puppy's best health-insurance policy. If you do not already have a vet, ask your breeder, friends and experienced dog people in your area for recommendations so that you can select a vet before you bring your Standard Schnauzer puppy home. Also arrange for your puppy's first veterinary examination beforehand, since many vets do not have appointments available immediately, and your puppy should visit the vet within a day or so of coming home.

It's important to make sure that your puppy's first visit to the vet is a pleasant and positive one. The vet should take great care to befriend the pup and handle him gently to make their first meeting a positive experience. The vet will give the pup a thorough physical examination and set up a schedule for vaccinations and other necessary wellness visits. Be sure to show your vet any health and inoculation records, which you should have received from your breeder. Your vet is a great source of canine health information, so be sure to ask questions and take notes. Creating a health journal for your puppy will make a handy reference for his wellness and any future health problems that may arise.

ARE VACCINATIONS NECESSARY?

Vaccinations are recommended for all puppies by the American Veterinary Medical Association (AVMA). Some vaccines are absolutely necessary, while others depend upon a dog's or puppy's individual exposure to certain diseases or the animal's immune history. Rabies vaccinations are required by law in all 50 states. Some diseases are fatal whereas others are treatable, making the need for vaccinating against the latter questionable. Follow your veterinarian's recommendations to keep your dog fully immunized and protected. You can also review the AVMA directive on vaccinations on their website: www.avma.org.

MEETING THE FAMILY

Your Standard Schnauzer's homecoming is an exciting time for all members of the family, and it's only natural that everyone will be eager to meet him, pet him and play with him. However, for the puppy's sake, it's best to make these initial family meetings as uneventful as possible so that the pup is not overwhelmed with too much too soon. Remember, he has just left his dam and his littermates and is away from the breeder's home for the first time. Despite his fuzzy wagging tail, he is still apprehensive and wondering where he is and who all these strange humans are. It's best to let him explore on his own and meet the family members as he feels comfortable. Let him investigate all the new smells, sights and sounds at his own pace. Children should be especially careful to not get overly excited, use loud voices or hug the pup too tightly. Be calm, gentle and affectionate, and be ready to comfort him if he appears frightened or uneasy.

Be sure to show your puppy his new crate during this first day home. Toss a treat or two inside the crate; if he associates the crate with food, he will associate the crate with good things. If he is comfortable with the crate, you can offer him his first meal inside it. Leave the door ajar so he can wander in and out as he chooses.

TOXIC PLANTS

Plants are natural puppy magnets, but many can be harmful, even fatal, if ingested by a puppy or adult dog. Scout your yard and home interior and remove any plants, bushes or flowers that could be even mildly dangerous. It could save your puppy's life. You can obtain a complete list of toxic plants from your veterinarian, at the public library or by looking online.

FIRST NIGHT IN HIS NEW HOME

So much has happened in your Standard Schnauzer puppy's first day away from the breeder. He's had his first car ride to his new home. He's met his new human family and perhaps the other family pets. He has explored his new house and yard, at least those places where he is to be allowed during his first weeks at

An experienced breeder will be able to make sensible judgments about matching pups to new owners.

home. He may have visited his new veterinarian. He has eaten his first meal or two away from his dam and littermates. Surely that's enough to tire out a young Standard Schnauzer pup—or so you hope!

It's bedtime. During the day, the pup investigated his crate, which is his new den and sleeping space, so it is not entirely strange to him. Line the crate with a soft towel or blanket that he can snuggle into and gently place him into the crate for the night. Some breeders send

Take it slow when your new pup first comes home; let him warm up to each family member gradually.

home a piece of bedding from where the pup slept with his littermates, and those familiar scents are a great comfort for the puppy on his first night without his siblings.

He will probably whine or cry. The puppy is objecting to the confinement and the fact that he is alone for the first time. This can be a stressful time for you as well as for the pup. It's important that you remain strong and don't let the puppy out of his crate to comfort him. He will fall asleep eventually. If you release him, the puppy will learn that crying means "out" and will continue that habit. You are laying the groundwork for future habits. Some breeders find that soft music can soothe a crying pup and help him get to sleep.

SOCIALIZING YOUR PUPPY
The first 20 weeks of your Standard Schnauzer puppy's life are the most important of his entire lifetime. A properly socialized puppy will grow up to be a confident and stable adult who will be a pleasure to live with and a welcome addition to the neighborhood. The importance of socialization cannot be overemphasized. Research on canine behavior has proven that puppies who are not exposed to new sights, sounds, people and animals during their first 20 weeks of life will grow up to be timid and fearful, even aggressive, and

unable to flourish outside of their home environment.

Socializing your puppy is not difficult and, in fact, will be a fun time for you both. Lead training goes hand in hand with socialization, so your puppy will be learning how to walk on a lead at the same time that he's meeting the neighborhood. Because the Standard Schnauzer is such a fascinating breed, everyone will enjoy meeting "the new kid on the block." Take him for short walks to the park and to other dog-friendly places where he will encounter new people, especially children. Puppies automatically recognize children as "little people" and are drawn to play with them. Just make sure that you supervise these meetings and that the children do not get too rough or encourage him to play too hard. An overzealous pup can often nip too hard, frightening the child and in turn making the puppy overly excited. A bad experience in

puppyhood can impact a dog for life, so a pup that has a negative experience with a child may grow up to be shy or even aggressive around children.

Take your puppy along on your daily errands. Puppies are natural "people magnets," and most people who see your pup will want to pet him. All of these encounters will help to mold him into a confident adult dog. Likewise, you will soon feel like a confident, responsible dog owner,

Once you've picked the perfect pup, the fun begins!

FINDING A QUALIFIED BREEDER

Before you begin your puppy search, ask for references from your veterinarian, other owners and other breeders to refer you to someone they believe is reputable. Responsible breeders usually raise only one or two breeds of dog. Avoid any breeder who has several different breeds or has several litters at the same time. Dedicated breeders are usually involved with a breed or other dog club. Many participate in some sport or activity related to their breed. Just as you want to be assured of the breeder's qualifications, the breeder wants to be assured that you will make a worthy owner. Expect the breeder to interview you, asking questions about your goals for the pup, your experience with dogs and what kind of home you will provide.

With a personality as irresistible as his fuzzy face, a Standard Schnauzer puppy is a born charmer.

during this time should be gentle and positive. A frightening or negative event could leave a permanent impression that could affect his future behavior if a similar situation arises.

Also make sure that your puppy has received his first and second rounds of vaccinations before you expose him to other dogs or bring him to places that other dogs may frequent. Avoid dog parks and other strange-dog areas until your vet assures you that your puppy is fully immunized and resistant to the diseases that can be passed between canines. Discuss safe socialization with your breeder and vet, as some recommend socializing the puppy even before he has received all of his inoculations, depending on the individual puppy.

rightly proud of your mannerly Standard Schnauzer.

If you have your pup at this age, be especially careful of his encounters and experiences during the eight-to-ten-week-old period, which is also called the "fear period." This is a serious imprinting period, and all contact

LEADER OF THE PUPPY'S PACK

Like other canines, your puppy needs an authority figure, someone he can look up to and regard as the leader of his "pack." His first pack leader was his dam, who taught him to be polite and not to chew too hard on her ears or nip at her muzzle. He learned those same lessons from his littermates. If he played too rough, they cried in pain and stopped the game, which sent an important message to the rowdy puppy.

As puppies play together, they are also struggling to determine

REPEAT YOURSELF

Puppies learn best through repetition. Use the same verbal cues and commands when teaching your puppy new behaviors or correcting for misbehaviors. Be consistent, but not monotonous. Puppies get bored just like puppy owners.

who will be the boss. Being pack animals, dogs need someone to be in charge. If a litter of puppies remained together beyond puppyhood, one of the pups would emerge as the strongest one, the one who calls the shots.

Once your puppy leaves the pack, he will look intuitively for a new leader. If he does not recognize you as that leader, he will try to assume that position for himself. Of course, it is hard to imagine your adorable Standard

Doug Fisher and his friend Igor are ready to cruise in style.

THE FIRST FAMILY MEETING

Your puppy's first day at home should be quiet and uneventful. Despite his wagging tail, he is still wondering where his mom and siblings are! Let him make friends with other members of the family on his own terms; don't overwhelm him. You have a lifetime ahead to get to know each other!

Schnauzer puppy trying to be in charge when he is so small and seemingly helpless. You must remember that these are natural canine instincts. Do not cave in and allow your pup to get the upper "paw"!

Just as socialization is so important during these first 20 weeks, so too is your puppy's early education. He was born without any bad habits. He does not know what is good or bad behavior. If he does things like nipping and digging, it's because

he is having fun and doesn't know that humans consider these things as "bad." It's your job to teach him proper puppy manners, and this is the best time to accomplish that…before he has developed bad habits, since it is much more difficult to "unlearn" or correct unacceptable learned behavior than to teach good behavior from the start.

Make sure that all members of

Family fun is more fun with a Standard Schnauzer, and you can be sure that your dog will be up for joining you in as much as he can.

Love, care and affection from the start create the special lifelong bond between a dog and his family.

the family understand the importance of being consistent when training their new puppy. If you tell the puppy to stay off the sofa and your daughter allows him to cuddle on the couch to watch her favorite television show, your pup will be confused about what he is and is not allowed to do. Have a family conference before your pup comes home so that everyone understands the basic principles of puppy training and the rules you have set forth for the pup, and agrees to follow them.

The old saying that "an ounce of prevention is worth a pound of cure" is especially true when it comes to puppies. It is much easier to prevent inappropriate behavior than it is to change it. It's also easier and less stressful for the pup, since it will keep discipline to a minimum and create a more positive learning environment for him. That, in turn, will also be easier on you.

Here are a few commonsense tips to keep your belongings safe and your puppy out of trouble:

- Keep your closet doors closed and your shoes, socks and other apparel off the floor so your puppy can't get at them.
- Keep a secure lid on the trash container or put the trash where your puppy can't dig into it. He can't damage what he can't reach!
- Supervise your puppy at all times to make sure he is not getting into mischief. If he starts to chew the corner of the rug, you can distract him instantly by tossing a toy for him to fetch. You also will be able to whisk him outside when you notice that he is about to piddle on the carpet. If you can't see your puppy, you can't teach him or correct his behavior after the fact.

TEETHING TIME

All puppies chew. It's normal canine behavior. Chewing just plain feels good to a puppy, especially during the three- to five-month teething period when the adult teeth are breaking through the gums. Rather than attempting to eliminate such a strong natural chewing instinct, you will be more successful if you redirect it and teach your puppy what he may or may not chew. Correct inappropriate chewing with a sharp "No!" and offer him a chew toy, praising him when he takes it. Don't become discouraged. Chewing usually decreases after the adult teeth have come in.

SOLVING PUPPY PROBLEMS

CHEWING AND NIPPING

Nipping at fingers and toes is normal puppy behavior. Chewing is also the way that puppies investigate their surroundings. However, you will have to teach your puppy that chewing anything other than his toys is not acceptable. That won't happen overnight and at times puppy teeth will test your patience. However, if you allow nipping and chewing to continue, just think about the damage that a mature Standard Schnauzer can do with a full set of adult teeth.

Whenever your puppy nips your hand or fingers, cry out "Ouch!" in a loud voice, which should startle your puppy and stop him from nipping, even if only for a moment. Immediately distract him by offering a small treat or an appropriate toy for him to chew instead (which means having chew toys and puppy treats handy or in your pockets at all times). Praise him when he takes the toy and tell him what a good fellow he is. Praise is just as or even more important in puppy training as discipline and correction.

Puppies also tend to nip at children more often than adults, since they perceive little ones to be more vulnerable and more similar to their littermates. Teach your children appropriate

A Standard Schnauzer can make short work of a big stick, so be careful about what your dog chews, especially items that can splinter and break.

responses to nipping behavior. If they are unable to handle it themselves, you may have to intervene. Puppy nips can be quite painful and a child's frightened reaction will only encourage a puppy to nip harder, which is a natural canine response. As with all other puppy situations, interaction between your Standard Schnauzer

If you don't provide your Standard Schnauzer with appropriate chew items, he will be happy to help himself to whatever he can find.

From the farm to the dog park, your Standard Schnauzer will thrive as long as he is part of your life. Your canine companion wants to share in as much of what you do as possible.

The best solution is, once again, prevention. If you value something, keep it tucked away and out of reach. You can't hide your dining-room table in a closet, but you can try to deflect the chewing by applying a bitter product made just to deter dogs from chewing. This spray-on substance is vile-tasting, although safe for dogs, and most puppies will avoid the forbidden object after one tiny taste. You also can apply the product to your leather leash if the puppy tries to chew on his lead during leash-training sessions.

Keep a ready supply of safe chews handy to offer your Standard Schnauzer as a distraction when he starts to chew on something that's a "no-no." Remember, at this tender age he does not yet know what is permitted or forbidden, so you have to be "on call" every minute he's awake and on the prowl.

You may lose a treasure or two during puppy's growing-up period, and the furniture could sustain a nasty nick or two. These can be trying times, so be prepared for those inevitable accidents and comfort yourself in knowing that this too shall pass.

puppy and children should be supervised.

Chewing on objects, not just family members' fingers and ankles, is also normal canine behavior that can be especially tedious (for the owner, not the pup) during the teething period when the puppy's adult teeth are coming in. At this stage, chewing just plain feels good. Furniture legs and cabinet corners are common puppy favorites. Shoes and other personal items also taste pretty good to a pup.

JUMPING UP

Many Standard Schnauzers feel that it is their job in the household to be the official "jump-greet-licker" to all guests. To the dog's way of thinking, this is the best way of saying "Hi!" If you feel that guests to your home will not appreciate this type of greeting, then you must stop this behavior in your pup before it becomes an ingrained habit in your adult dog.

The key to jump correction is consistency. You cannot correct your Standard Schnauzer for jumping up on you today, then allow it to happen tomorrow by greeting him with hugs and kisses. As you have learned by now, consistency is critical to all puppy lessons.

For starters, try turning your back as soon as the puppy jumps. Jumping up is a means of gaining your attention and, if the pup can't see your face, he may get discouraged and learn that he loses eye contact with his beloved master when he jumps up.

Leash corrections also work, and most puppies respond well to a leash tug if they jump. Grasp the leash close to the puppy's collar and give a quick tug downward, using the command "Off." Do not use the word "Down," since "Down" is used to teach the puppy to lie down, which is a separate action that he will learn during his education in the basic commands. As soon as the puppy has backed off, tell him to sit and immediately praise him for doing so. This will take many repetitions and won't be accomplished quickly, so don't get discouraged or give up; you must be even more persistent than your puppy.

A second method used for jump correction is the spritzer bottle. Fill a spray bottle with water mixed with a bit of lemon juice or vinegar. As soon as puppy jumps, command him "Off" and spritz him with the water mixture. Of course, that means having the spray bottle handy whenever or wherever jumping usually happens.

Yet a third method to discourage jumping is grasping the

While most Standard Schnauzer owners appreciate a jumping, hugging hello from their dogs, will everyone you meet feel the same way?

puppy's paws and holding them gently but firmly until he struggles to get away. Wait a brief moment or two, then release his paws and give him a command to sit. He should eventually learn that jumping gets him into an uncomfortable predicament.

Children are major victims of puppy jumping, since puppies view little people as ready targets for jumping up as well as nipping. If your children (or their friends) are unable to dispense jump corrections, you will have to intervene and handle it for them.

Important to prevention is also knowing what you should not do. Never kick your Standard Schnauzer (for any reason, not just for jumping) or knock him in the chest with your knee. That maneuver could actually harm your puppy. Vets can tell you stories about puppies who suffered broken bones after being banged about when they jumped up.

Puppy Whining

Puppies often cry and whine, just as infants and little children do. It's their way of telling us that they are lonely or in need of attention. Your puppy will miss his littermates and will feel insecure when he is left alone. You may be out of the house or just in another room, but he will still feel alone. During these times, the puppy's crate should be his personal comfort station, a place all his own where he can feel safe and

secure. Once he learns that being alone is okay and not something to be feared, he will settle down without crying or objecting. You might want to leave a radio on while he is crated, as the sound of human voices can be soothing and will give the impression that people are around.

Give your puppy a favorite cuddly toy or chew toy to entertain him whenever he is crated. You will both be happier: the puppy because he is safe in his den and you because he is quiet, safe and not getting into puppy escapades that can wreak havoc in your house or cause him danger.

To make sure that your puppy will always view his crate as a safe and cozy place, never, *ever*, use the crate as punishment. That's the best way to turn the crate into a negative place that the pup will want to avoid. Sure, you can use the crate for your own peace of mind if your puppy is getting into trouble and needs some "time out." Just don't let him know that! Never scold the pup and immediately place him into the crate. Count to ten, give him a couple of hugs and maybe a treat, then scoot him into his crate.

It's also important not to make a big fuss when he is released from the crate. That will make getting out of the crate more appealing than being in the crate, which is just the opposite of what you are trying to achieve.

STANDARD SCHNAUZER

Adding a Standard Schnauzer to your household means adding a new family member who will need your care each and every day. When your Standard Schnauzer pup first comes home, you will start a routine with him so that, as he grows up, your dog will have a daily schedule just as you do. The aspects of your dog's daily care will likewise become regular parts of your day, so you'll both have a new schedule. Dogs learn by consistency and thrive on routine: regular times for meals, exercise, grooming and potty trips are just as important for your dog as they are for you! Your dog's schedule will depend much on your family's daily routine, but remember that you now have a new member of the family who is part of your day every day.

FEEDING

Feeding your dog the best diet is based on various factors, including age, activity level, overall condition and size of breed. When you visit the breeder, he will share with you his advice about the proper diet for your dog based on his experience with the breed and the foods with which he has had success. Likewise, your vet will be a helpful source of advice throughout the dog's life and will aid you in planning a diet for optimal health.

FEEDING THE PUPPY

Of course, your pup's very first food will be his dam's milk. There may be special situations in which pups fail to nurse, necessitating

---

VARIETY IS THE SPICE

Although dog-food manufacturers contend that dogs don't like variety in their diets, studies show quite the opposite to be true. Dogs would much rather vary their meals than eat the same old chow day in and day out. Dry kibble is no more exciting for a dog than the same bowl of bran flakes would be for you. Fortunately, there are dozens of varieties available on the market, and your dog will likely show preference for certain flavors over others. A word of warning: don't make changes too often. You could upset your dog's stomach or you may develop a fussy eater who only prefers chopped beef fillet and asparagus tips every night.

that the breeder hand-feed them with a formula, but for the most part pups spend the first weeks of life nursing from their dam. The breeder weans the pups by gradually introducing solid foods and decreasing the milk meals. Pups may even start themselves off on the weaning process, albeit inadvertently, if they snatch bites from their mom's food bowl.

By the time the pups are ready for new homes, they are fully weaned and eating a good puppy food. As a new owner, you may be thinking, "Great! The breeder has taken care of the hard part." Not so fast.

A puppy's first year of life is the time when most of his growth and development takes place. This is a delicate time, and diet plays a huge role in proper skeletal and muscular formation. Improper diet and exercise habits can lead to damaging problems that will compromise the dog's health and movement for his entire life. That being said, new owners should not worry needlessly. With the myriad

> ## SWITCHING FOODS
> There are certain times in a dog's life when it becomes necessary to switch his food; for example, from puppy to adult food and then from adult to senior-dog food. Additionally, you may decide to feed your pup a different type of food from what he received from the breeder, and there may be "emergency" situations in which you can't find your dog's normal brand and have to offer something else temporarily. Anytime a change is made, for whatever reason, the switch must be done gradually. You don't want to upset the dog's stomach or end up with a picky eater who refuses to eat something new. A tried-and-true approach is, over the course of about a week, to mix a little of the new food in with the old, increasing the proportion of new to old as the days progress. At the end of the week, you'll be feeding his regular portions of the new food, and he will barely notice the change.

Feeding a hungry litter is no small task, but this doting mom is up to the challenge.

types of food formulated specifically for growing pups of different-sized breeds, dog-food manufacturers have taken much of the guesswork out of feeding your puppy well. Since growth-food formulas are designed to provide the nutrition that a growing puppy needs, it is unnecessary and, in fact, can prove harmful to add supplements to the diet. Research has shown that too much of certain vitamin supplements and minerals predispose a dog to skeletal problems. It's by no means a case of "if a little is good, a lot is better." At every stage of your dog's life, too much or too little in the way of nutrients can be harmful, which is why a manufactured complete food is the easiest way to know that your dog is getting what he needs.

Because of a young pup's small body and accordingly small digestive system, his daily portion will be divided up into small meals throughout the day. This can mean starting off with three or more meals a day and decreasing the number of meals as the pup matures. For the adult Standard Schnauzer, dividing the day's food into two meals on a morning/ evening schedule is healthier for the dog's digestion than one large daily portion.

Regarding the feeding schedule, feeding the pup at the same times and in the same place each day is important for both housebreaking purposes and establishing the dog's everyday routine. As for the amount to feed, growing puppies generally need proportionately more food per body weight than their adult counterparts, but a pup should never be allowed to gain excess weight. Dogs of all ages should be kept in proper body condition, but extra weight can strain a pup's developing frame, causing skeletal problems.

A good puppy food offers balanced nutrition to promote healthy growth and development.

Watch your pup's weight as he grows and, if the recommended amounts seem to be too much or too little for your pup, consult the vet about appropriate dietary changes. Keep in mind that treats, although small, can quickly add up throughout the day, contributing unnecessary calories. Treats are fine when used

Dinnertime for a Standard Schnauzer litter. The breeder introduces the pups to solid foods and they should be fully weaned when they go to new homes.

Adult and puppy Standard Schnauzers should have different diets, though pups will certainly stick their noses into mom's bowl.

prudently; opt for dog treats specially formulated to be healthy or for nutritious snacks like small pieces of cheese or cooked chicken.

FEEDING THE ADULT DOG

For the adult (meaning physically mature) dog, feeding properly is about maintenance, not growth. In general, the diet of a Standard Schnauzer can be changed to an adult one at about eight to ten months of age, as by this age the dog will have reached most of his mature height and weight. One exception is the puppy who is too hyperactive and not getting enough exercise; this pup can be switched earlier to an adult food with fewer calories and less energy-producing fat and protein.

At every stage of life, correct weight is a concern. Your dog should appear fit and should have an evident "waist." His ribs should not be protruding (a sign of being underweight), but they should be covered by only a slight

layer of fat. Under normal circumstances, an adult dog can be maintained fairly easily with a high-quality nutritionally complete adult-formula food.

Factor treats into your dog's overall daily caloric intake, and avoid offering table scraps. Not only are certain "people foods," like chocolate, nuts, grapes, raisins, onions and considerable amounts of garlic, toxic to dogs but feeding from your plate also encourages begging and overeating. Overweight dogs are more prone to health problems. Research has even shown that obesity takes years off a dog's life. With that in mind, resist the urge to overfeed and over-treat. Don't make unnecessary additions to your dog's diet, whether with tidbits or with extra vitamins and minerals. There are special food formulas designed for dogs that tend to be overweight.

HOLD THE ONIONS

Sliced, chopped or grated; dehydrated, boiled, fried or raw; pearl, Spanish, white or red: onions can be deadly to your dog. The toxic effects of onions in dogs are cumulative for up to 30 days. A serious form of anemia, called Heinz body anemia, affects the red blood cells of dogs that have eaten onions. For safety (and better breath), dogs should avoid chives and scallions as well.

Most Standard Schnauzers seem to have stomachs of cast iron and can take changes in diet easily. Sometimes you will find one with a very sensitive stomach that has to be introduced to new food very slowly. A lot of them, when given the chance, will relish the opportunity to eat new grass. I had one that had a passion for Zinnia plants. Needless to say, grass and Zinnia plants are not recommended diets.

The Standard Schnauzer is usually not a picky eater. Most eat their food like they were four-legged vacuum cleaners. The amount of food varies with each dog, ranging from one-and-a-half cups a day for an inactive "couch potato" to three to four cups a day for an extremely active dog. The average, which works for most adult Standard Schnauzers, is one cup twice a day.

While the amount of food needed for proper maintenance will vary depending on your individual dog's activity level, you will be able to tell whether the daily portions are keeping him in good shape. With the wide variety of good complete foods available, choosing what to feed is largely a matter of personal preference. Just as with the puppy, the adult dog should have consistency in his mealtimes and feeding place. In addition to a consistent routine, regular mealtimes also allow the owner to see how much his dog is eating. If the dog seems never to be satisfied or, likewise, becomes uninterested in his food, the owner will know right away that something is wrong and can consult the vet. It is also wise for all dogs to have some quiet time before and after mealtimes, so this should be part of the feeding schedule too.

DIETS FOR THE AGING DOG

The Standard Schnauzer ages very well and is a very "youthful" dog for much longer than many other breeds its size. Whereas many breeds are started on "senior" food at six or seven years of age, most

NOT HUNGRY?
No dog in his right mind would turn down his dinner, would he? If you notice that your dog has lost interest in his food, there could be any number of causes. Dental problems are a common cause of appetite loss, one that is often overlooked. If your dog has a toothache, a loose tooth or sore gums from infection, chances are it doesn't feel so good to chew. Think about when you've had a toothache! If your dog does not approach the food bowl with his usual enthusiasm, look inside his mouth for signs of a problem. Whatever the cause, you'll want to consult your vet so that your chow hound can get back to his happy, hungry self as soon as possible.

Standard Schnauzer breeders do not put their dogs on senior food until nine or ten years of age. At this time, a change in diet becomes warranted.

What does aging have to do with your dog's diet? No, he won't get a discount at the local diner's early-bird special. Yes, he will require some dietary changes to accommodate the changes that come along with increased age. One change is that the older dog's dietary needs become more similar to that of a puppy. Specifically, dogs can metabolize more protein as youngsters and seniors than in the adult-maintenance stage. Discuss with your vet whether you need to switch to a higher-protein or senior-formulated food or

> **DIET DON'TS**
> • Got milk? Don't give it to your dog! Dogs cannot tolerate large quantities of cows' milk, as they do not have the enzymes to digest lactose.
> • You may have heard of dog owners who add raw eggs to their dogs' food for a shiny coat or to make the food more palatable, but consumption of raw eggs too often can cause a deficiency of the vitamin biotin.
> • Avoid feeding table scraps, as they will upset the balance of the dog's complete food. Additionally, fatty or highly seasoned foods can cause upset canine stomachs.
> • Vitamin A toxicity in dogs can be caused by too much raw liver, especially if the dog already gets enough vitamin A in his balanced diet, which should be the case.
> • Bones like chicken, pork chop and other soft bones are not suitable, as they easily splinter.

Water is the best thirst-quencher for dogs and should be readily available to your Standard Schnauzer.

whether your current adult-dog food contains sufficient nutrition for the senior.

Watching the dog's weight remains essential, even more so in the senior stage. Older dogs are already more vulnerable to illness, and obesity only contributes to their susceptibility to problems. As the older dog becomes less active and, thus, exercises less, his regular portions may cause him to

WHAT IS "BLOAT" AND HOW DO I PREVENT IT?

You likely have heard the term "bloat," which refers to gastric torsion (gastric dilatation/volvulus), a potentially fatal condition. As it is directly related to feeding and exercise practices, a brief explanation here is warranted. The term *dilatation* means that the dog's stomach is filled with air, while *volvulus* means that the stomach is twisted around on itself, blocking the entrance/exit points. Dilatation/volvulus is truly a deadly combination, although they also can occur independently of each other. An affected dog cannot digest food or pass gas, and blood cannot flow to the stomach, causing accumulation of toxins and gas along with great pain and rapidly occuring shock.

Many theories exist on what exactly causes bloat. We do know that deep-chested breeds are more prone, but no dog is immune. Activities like eating a large meal, gulping water, strenuous exercise too close to mealtimes or a combination of these factors can contribute to bloat, though not every case is directly related to these more well-known causes. With that in mind, we can focus on incorporating simple daily preventives and knowing how to recognize the symptoms. In addition to the tips presented in this book, ask your vet about how to prevent and recognize bloat. An affected dog needs immediate veterinary attention, as death can result quickly. Signs include obvious restlessness/discomfort, crying in pain, drooling/excessive salivation, unproductive attempts to vomit or relieve himself, visibly bloated appearance and collapsing. Do not wait: get to the vet *right away* if you see any of these symptoms. The vet will confirm by x-ray if the stomach is bloated with air; if so, the dog must be treated *immediately*.

As varied as the causes of bloat are the tips for prevention, but some common preventive methods follow:
• Feed two or three small meals daily rather than one large one;
• Moisten dry kibble with water and let stand for a few minutes before feeding;
• Never permit rapid eating or gulping of water;
• No exercise for the dog at least two hours before and (especially) after meals;
• Feed high-quality food with adequate protein, adequate fiber content and not too much fat and carbohydrate;
• Explore herbal additives, enzymes or gas-reduction products (only under a vet's advice) to encourage a "friendly" environment in the dog's digestive system;
• Avoid foods and ingredients known to produce gas;
• Avoid stressful situations for the dog, especially at mealtimes;
• Make dietary changes gradually, over a period of a few weeks;
• Do not feed dry food only;
• Although the role of genetics as a causative of bloat is not known, many breeders do not breed from previously affected dogs;
• Sometimes owners are advised to have gastroplexy (stomach stapling) performed on their dogs as a preventive measure;
• Pay attention to your dog's behavior and any changes that could be symptomatic of bloat. Your dog's life depends on it!

Enjoying a romp on the beach, Taylor and Stella agree that exercise is more fun with a friend.

gain weight. At this point, you may consider decreasing his daily food intake or switching to a reduced-calorie food. As with other changes, you should consult your vet for advice.

DON'T FORGET THE WATER!

For a dog, it's always time for a drink! Regardless of what type of food he eats, there's no doubt that he needs plenty of water. Fresh cold water, in a clean bowl, should be freely available to your dog. There are special circumstances, such as during puppy housebreaking, when you will want to monitor your pup's water intake so that you will be able to predict when he will need to relieve himself, but water must be available to him nonetheless. Water is essential for hydration and proper body function just as it is in humans.

You will get to know how much your dog typically drinks in a day. Of course, in the heat or if exercising vigorously, he will be more thirsty and will drink more. However, if he begins to drink noticeably more water for no apparent reason, this could signal any of various problems, and you are advised to consult your vet.

Water is the best drink for dogs. Some owners are tempted to give milk from time to time or to moisten dry food with milk, but dogs do not have the enzymes necessary to digest the lactose in milk, which is much different from the milk that nursing puppies receive. Therefore stick with clean fresh water to quench your dog's thirst, and always have it readily available to him.

EXERCISE

The amount of exercise that a Standard Schnauzer needs to be kept in top condition depends very much on the individual dog, but the breed as a whole does require moderate exercise. A Standard Schnauzer living in an apartment needs a minimum of three brisk walks of one to two miles per day to be kept in top physical condition. In a house environment, some Standard Schnauzers are self-motivated exercisers and will keep moving constantly, using any excuse available, especially if they have a playmate. On the other hand, there is the occasional "couch potato" that must be coaxed to exercise. If you do have a such a dog, a minimum of two very brisk half-hour daily walks is strongly recommended.

Walking is the most popular way to exercise a dog (it's good for you, too!); other suggestions include retrieving games, jogging and disc-catching or other active games with his toys. If you have a safe body of water nearby and a dog that likes to swim, swimming is an excellent form of exercise for dogs, putting no stress on their frames.

On that note, some precautions should be taken with a puppy's exercise. During his first year, when he is growing and developing, your Standard Schnauzer should not be subject to vigorous activity that stresses his body. Short walks at a comfortable pace and play sessions in the fenced yard are good for a growing pup, and his exercise can be increased as he grows up.

For overweight dogs, dietary changes and activity will help the goal of weight loss. (Sound familiar?) While they should of course be encouraged to be active, remember not to overdo it, as the excess weight is already putting strain on his vital organs and bones. As for highly active dogs, some of them never seem to tire! They will enjoy time spent with their owners, doing things together.

Regardless of your dog's condition and activity level, exercise offers benefits to all dogs and owners. Consider the fact that dogs who are kept active are more stimulated both physically and mentally, meaning that they are less likely to become bored and lapse into destructive behavior. Also consider the benefits of one-on-one time with your dog every day, continually strengthening the bond between the two of you. Furthermore, exercising together will improve health and longevity for both of you. You both need

Exercise is good for owner and Standard Schnauzer alike. A retractable lead is useful once the dog has been trained to walk nicely on a traditional lead.

Although not the preferred method of Standard Schnauzer people, machine-clipping is a satisfactory method for pet dogs. Electric clipping causes the coat to lose its characteristic coarseness and coloration.

exercise, and now you and your dog have a workout partner and motivator.

GROOMING THE STANDARD SCHNAUZER

Keeping up the "jacket" on the Standard Schnauzer is a relatively high-maintenance job if you are planning to show your dog. For the average Standard Schnauzer kept strictly as a companion and

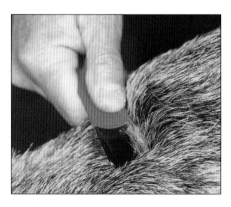

More time-intensive hand-stripping is the preferred method of maintaining a Standard Schnauzer's coat. Ask a professional groomer or your breeder how to properly use a stripping knife.

family pet, there are two options for maintaining the jacket. The easiest option is to take the dog to the local grooming parlor and have the body coat machine-clipped. The very distinctive leg furnishings, beard and eyebrows of the Standard Schnauzer do not shed like the jacket. They continue to grow and are always hand-scissored when the jacket is clipped. The Standard Schnauzer groomed this way requires a trip to the parlor every six to eight weeks. This method of grooming is much quicker, easier on the dog and most certainly easier on the purse.

Most breeders routinely machine-clip their old-timers that are no longer being shown. The one big drawback to this method is that in most cases the coat becomes much softer over the years. The characteristic pepper and salt coloration gradually fades out and turns to a solid gray. The black dogs gradually lose the shine to their coats, with some developing a brownish tinge.

The proper method of maintaining the Standard Schnauzer coat is to hand-strip the jacket. This is the way that the jacket is maintained in show dogs. If you choose this option, you must either learn how to hand-strip (pluck out) the harsh wiry outer topcoat yourself or find an experienced fellow owner, handler or breeder who is willing to teach you—or better yet, do it for you! Hand-stripping requires a minimum of twice-a-week maintenance in a dog being actively shown, or approximately two or three times a year, depending on the harshness of the coat, for the well-maintained pet. The furnishings (once again, depending on the texture) of the dog being maintained this way can either be done by hand with scissors or by hand-plucking only the longest hairs to tidy up the legs.

Hand-stripping or plucking of the jacket is the removal of the dead hair from the hair shaft. The hair is not cut. This method keeps the desirable hard, wiry texture of the jacket, which is one of the Standard Schnauzer's outstanding characteristics. The dog must be maintained in this fashion if he is being shown in the conformation ring, as the texture of the jacket is a very major consideration. In some parts of the world, breeders, in an attempt to make a prettier dog with more profuse leg and beard furnishings, do not pay as much attention to texture of the outer coat as they should.

These dogs are particularly hard to hand-strip. A very strong word of warning: be very careful when you first talk to a local all-breed groomer about grooming your Standard Schnauzer. Be very specific and request that the dog be "hand-stripped" or "plucked" if that is the method by which you wish your dog to be maintained. If

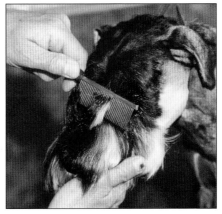

A strong steel-toothed comb with a gentle touch is very useful on the facial hair, especially around the muzzle to prevent food particles from accumulating.

you do not specifically use this terminology, you could return later to find that your dog has been machine-stripped (clipped) of *all* hair, including that on the muzzle, eyes and legs! And that makes for a very embarrassed and sad-looking Standard Schnauzer.

Whichever method is used to maintain the coat, a daily washing and combing of the beard is required to prevent build-up of food particles and to prevent

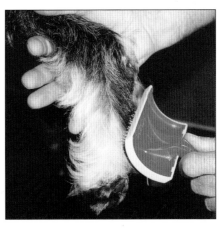

A slicker brush is used to brush out the leg furnishings.

doggy odors. The beard and leg furnishings should be combed out two or three times a week to prevent mats from forming. A brushing of the body coat with a stiff bristle brush twice a week will keep the skin and body coat in excellent condition and free of odors and dirt.

BATHING

Bathing too frequently can have negative effects on the skin and coat, removing natural oils and causing dryness as well as

softening the breed's desired harsh coat texture. Bathing the Standard Schnauzer is not necessary unless your dog decides to revert to his wild canine instincts of rolling in some horrible smelly mess that he considers to be perfume of the gods or if he starts to smell like a dog. Mary Moore (Odivane kennels) tells the story of six of her dogs, when out for a walk, jumping into a black muck ditch. When she pulled them out, all covered in the black muck, they didn't even recognize each other and at once started a fight. Needless to say, all dogs promptly went home and had a good bath.

If you give your dog his first bath when he is young, he will become accustomed to the process. Wrestling a dog into the tub or chasing a freshly shampooed dog who has escaped from the bath will be no fun! Most dogs don't naturally enjoy their baths, but you at least want yours to cooperate with you.

Before bathing the dog, have the items you'll need close at hand. First, decide where you will bathe the dog. You should have a tub or basin with a non-slip surface. Puppies can even be bathed in a sink. In warm weather, some like to use a portable pool in the yard, although you'll want to make sure that your dog doesn't head for the nearest dirt pile following his bath! You will also need a hose or shower spray to wet

---

WATER SHORTAGE

No matter how well behaved your dog is, bathing is always a project! Nothing can substitute for a good warm bath, but owners do have the option of giving their dogs "dry" baths. Pet shops sell excellent products, in both powder and spray forms, designed for spot-cleaning your dog. These dry shampoos are convenient for touch-up jobs when you don't have the time to bathe your dog in the traditional way.

Muddy feet, messy behinds and smelly coats can be spot-cleaned and deodorized with a "wet-nap"-style cleaner. On those days when your dog insists on rolling in fresh goose droppings and there's no time for a bath, a spot bath can save the day. These pre-moistened wipes are also handy for other grooming needs like wiping faces, ears and eyes and freshening tails and behinds.

the coat thoroughly, a shampoo formulated for dogs and several absorbent towels. Human shampoos are too harsh for dogs' coats and will dry them out.

Before wetting the dog, give him a brush-through to remove any dead hair, dirt and mats. Make sure he is at ease in the tub and have the water at a comfortable temperature. Begin bathing by wetting the coat all the way down to the skin. Massage in the shampoo, keeping it away from his face and eyes. Rinse him thoroughly, again avoiding the eyes and ears, as you don't want to get water into the ear canals. A thorough rinsing is important, as shampoo residue is drying and itchy to the dog. After rinsing, wrap him in a towel to absorb the initial moisture. You can finish drying with another towel, combing or brushing to smooth down the coat as it dries and prevent it from sticking out every which way. You should keep the dog indoors and away from drafts until he is completely dry.

For a dog that has had a run-in with a skunk, mix a solution of 1 quart 3% hydrogen peroxide, 1/4 cup baking soda and 1 teaspoon liquid dish detergent. Apply the mixture thoroughly to the dog's coat and then rinse him well with regular tap water. This remedy comes highly recommended for all dogs, and many a Standard Schnauzer owner has found it very helpful.

NAIL CLIPPING

Having his nails trimmed is not on many dogs' lists of favorite things to do. With this in mind, you will need to accustom your puppy to the procedure at a young age so that he will sit still (well, as still as he can) for his pedicures. Long nails can cause the dog's feet to spread, which is not good for him; likewise, long nails can hurt if they unintentionally scratch, not good for you!

Some dogs' nails are worn down naturally by regular walking on hard surfaces, so the frequency with which you clip depends on your individual dog. Look at his nails from time to time and clip as needed; a good way to know when it's time for a trim is if you hear your dog clicking as he walks across the floor.

There are several types of nail clippers and even electric nail-grinding tools made for dogs; first

The guillotine-style nail clipper is relatively easy to use, but you still must be very careful not to cut into the quick.

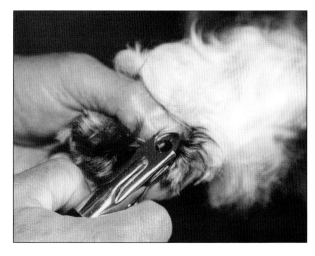

NAIL-GRINDING TIP

If using a nail grinder, here's a helpful hint: take a pair of pantyhose and stick the nail that you are working on through the mesh of the hose. This will enable to you trim the nail while keeping the dog's leg furnishings protected from getting caught in the grinder. If not protected, the leg hair can easily become caught, and this would be quite a painful experience for the dog.

we'll discuss using the clipper. To start, have your clipper ready and some doggie treats on hand. You want your pup to view his nail-clipping sessions in a positive light, and what better way to convince him than with food? You may want to enlist the help of an assistant to comfort the pup and offer treats as you concentrate on

the clipping itself. The guillotine-type clipper is thought of by many as the easiest type to use; the nail tip is inserted into the opening, and blades on the top and bottom snip it off in one clip.

Start by grasping the pup's paw; a little pressure on the foot pad causes the nail to extend, making it easier to clip. Clip off a little at a time. If you can see the "quick," which is a blood vessel that runs through each nail, you will know how much to trim, as you do not want to cut into the quick. On that note, if you do cut the quick, which will cause bleeding, you can stem the flow of blood with a styptic pencil or other clotting agent. If you mistakenly nip the quick, do not panic or fuss, as this will cause the pup to be afraid. Simply reassure the pup, stop the bleeding and move on to the next nail. Don't be discouraged; you will become a professional canine pedicurist with practice.

You may or may not be able to see the quick, so it's best to just clip off a small bit at a time. If you see a dark dot in the center of the nail, this is the quick and your cue to stop clipping. Tell the puppy he's a "good boy" and offer a piece of treat with each nail. You can also use nail-clipping time to examine the footpads, making sure that they are not dry and cracked and that nothing has become embedded in them.

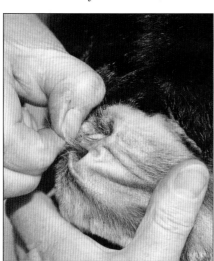

Excess hair in the ear can be plucked out easily, causing no pain to the dog.

The nail grinder, the other choice, is many owners' first choice. Accustoming the puppy to the sound of the grinder and sensation of the buzz presents fewer challenges than the clipper, and there's no chance of cutting through the quick. Use the grinder on a low setting and always talk soothingly to your dog. He won't mind his salon visit, and he'll have nicely polished nails as well.

EAR CLEANING

While keeping your dog's ears clean unfortunately will not cause him to "hear" your commands any better, it will protect him from ear infection and ear-mite infestation. In addition, a dog's ears are vulnerable to waxy build-up and to collecting foreign matter from the outdoors. Look in your dog's ears regularly to ensure that they look pink, clean and otherwise healthy. Even if they look fine, an odor in the ears signals a problem and means it's time to call the vet.

A dog's ears should be cleaned regularly; once a week is suggested, and you can do this along with your regular brushing of the coat. Using a cotton ball or pad, and never probing into the ear canal, wipe the ear gently. You can use an ear-cleansing liquid or powder available from your vet or pet-supply store.

Keep your dog's ears free of excess hair by plucking it as needed. If done gently, this will be painless for the dog. Look for wax, brown droppings (a sign of ear mites), redness or any other abnormalities. At the first sign of a problem, contact your vet so that he can prescribe an appropriate medication.

EYE CARE

During grooming sessions, pay extra attention to the condition of your dog's eyes. If the area around the eyes is soiled or if tear staining has occurred, there are various cleaning agents made especially for this purpose. Look at the dog's eyes to make sure no debris has entered; dogs with large eyes and those who spend time outdoors are especially prone to this.

The signs of an eye infection are obvious: mucus, redness, puffiness, scabs or other signs of irritation. If your dog's eyes become infected, the vet will likely prescribe an antibiotic

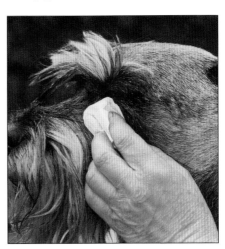

The areas around the eyes can be cleaned gently with a soft cloth and suitable cleansing formula made for the eye area.

Your Standard Schnauzer's teeth should be sparkling white and clean.

ointment for treatment. If you notice signs of more serious problems, such as opacities in the eye, which usually indicate cataracts, consult the vet at once. Taking time to pay attention to your dog's eyes will alert you in the early stages of any problem so that you can get your dog treatment as soon as possible. You could save your dog's sight!

A CLEAN SMILE

Another essential part of grooming is brushing your dog's teeth and checking his overall oral condition. Studies show that

Use dental-care products made for dogs when caring for your Standard Schnauzer's teeth.

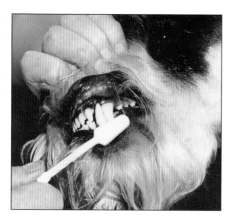

around 80% of dogs experience dental problems by two years of age, and the percentage is higher in older dogs. Therefore it is highly likely that your dog will have trouble with his teeth and gums unless you are proactive with home dental care.

The most common dental problem in dogs is plaque build-up. If not treated, this causes gum disease, infection and resultant tooth loss. Bacteria from these infections spread throughout the body, affecting the vital organs. Do you need much more convincing to start brushing your dog's teeth? If so, take a good whiff of your dog's breath and read on.

Although the Standard Schnauzer is blessed with strong teeth and gums, many dogs will develop plaque on their teeth as they grow older if given a lot of soft food. By brushing the teeth daily or at least weekly and making sure the dog has a variety of hard objects to chew on, trips to the veterinary clinic for major tooth cleanings can be greatly reduced. The vet should perform a thorough dental exam and perhaps a tooth scraping if needed at your dog's annual physical exam.

Introduce your pup to weekly toothbrushing as a routine part of grooming. Brushing can be done with a doggie toothbrush, a soft baby toothbrush or several layers of gauze wrapped around your finger. You can use a toothpaste formulated for dogs, or just moisten the brush or gauze with plain water and lightly scrub each tooth on the top and bottom jaws to remove the plaque.

THE OTHER END

Dogs sometime have troubles with their anal glands, which are sacs located beside the anal vent. These should empty when a dog has normal bowel movements; if they don't, they can become full or impacted, causing discomfort. Owners often are alarmed to see their dogs scooting across the floor, dragging their behinds behind; this is just a dog's attempt to empty the glands himself.

Some brave owners attempt to evacuate their dogs' anal glands themselves during grooming, but no one will tell you that this is a pleasant task! Thus, many owners prefer to make the trip to the vet to have the vet take care of the problem; owners whose dogs visit a groomer can have this done by the groomer if he offers this as part of his services. Regardless, don't neglect the dog's other end in your home-care routine. Look for scooting, licking or other signs of discomfort "back there" to ascertain whether the anal glands need to be emptied.

IDENTIFICATION FOR YOUR STANDARD SCHNAUZER

You love your Standard Schnauzer and want to keep him safe. Of

PET OR STRAY?
Besides the obvious benefit of providing your contact information to whoever finds your lost dog, an ID tag makes your dog more approachable and more likely to be recovered. A strange dog wandering the neighborhood without a collar and tags will look like a stray, while the collar and tags indicate that the dog is someone's pet. Even if the ID tags become detached from the collar, the collar alone will make a person more likely to pick up the dog.

course you take every precaution to prevent his escaping from the yard or becoming lost or stolen. You have a sturdy high fence and you always keep your dog on lead when out and about in public places. If your dog is not properly identified, however, you are overlooking a major aspect of his safety. We hope to never be in a situation where our dog is missing, but we should practice prevention in the unfortunate case that this happens; identification greatly increases the chances of your dog's being returned to you.

There are several ways to identify your dog. First, the traditional dog tag should be a staple in your dog's wardrobe, attached to his everyday collar. Tags can be made of sturdy plastic and various metals and should

Once accustomed to his crate, your dog will gladly travel in it. Your dog must be safely confined for rides in the car.

have fun and create a tag to match your dog's personality. Of course, it is important that the tag stays on the collar, so have a secure "O" ring attachment; you also can explore the type of tag that slides right onto the collar.

In addition to the ID tag, which every dog should wear even if identified by another method, two other forms of identification have become popular: microchipping and tattooing. In microchipping, a tiny scannable chip is painlessly inserted under the dog's skin. The number is registered to you so that, if your lost dog turns up at a clinic or shelter, the chip can be scanned to retrieve your contact information.

include your contact information so that a person who finds the dog can get in touch with you right away to arrange his return. Many people today enjoy the wide range of decorative tags available, so

The advantage of the microchip is that it is a permanent form of ID, but there are some factors to consider. Several different companies make microchips, and not all are compatible with the others' scanning devices. It's best to find a company with a universal microchip that can be read by scanners made by other companies as well. It won't do any good to have the dog chipped if the information cannot be retrieved. Also, not every humane society, shelter and clinic is equipped with a scanner, although more and more facilities are equipping themselves. In fact, many

CAR CAUTION

You may like to bring your canine companion along on the daily errands, but if you will be running in and out from place to place and can't bring him indoors with you, leave him at home. Your dog should never be left alone in the car, not even for a minute—never! A car heats up very quickly, and even a cracked-open window will not help. In fact, leaving the window cracked will be dangerous if the dog becomes uncomfortable and tries to escape. A dog left alone in a car can also be a target for dog thieves. When in doubt, leave your dog at home, where you know he will be safe.

shelters microchip dogs that they adopt out to new homes.

Because the microchip is not visible to the eye, the dog must wear a tag that states that he is microchipped so that whoever picks him up will know to have him scanned. The microchip tag usually also includes the registry's phone number and the dog's microchip ID number. He of course also should have a tag with your contact information in case his information cannot be retrieved. Humane societies and veterinary clinics offer microchipping service, which is usually very affordable.

Though less popular than microchipping, tattooing is another permanent method of ID for dogs. Most vets perform this

service, and there are also clinics that perform dog tattooing. This is also an affordable procedure and one that will not cause much discomfort for the dog. It is best to put the tattoo in a visible area, such as the ear, to deter theft. It is sad to say that there are cases of dogs' being stolen and sold to research laboratories, but such laboratories will not accept tattooed dogs.

To ensure that the tattoo is effective in aiding your dog's return to you, the tattoo number must be registered with a national organization. That way, when someone finds a tattooed dog, a phone call to the registry will quickly match the dog with his owner.

You should research and visit local boarding kennels well in advance of needing one so that you can be confident about the care your dog will receive if you need to board him.

TRAINING YOUR

STANDARD SCHNAUZER

As your Standard Schnauzer puppy grows up, you will have to make some decisions about the education of your new charge. This highly intelligent dog, if left in charge of his own upbringing, will very quickly take over the day-to-day running of your household. It is recommended that every Standard Schnauzer have some form of formal obedience training. This is almost mandatory for the first-time Standard Schnauzer owner, as the first two years of this breed's life can be very trying, even to the seasoned Standard Schnauzer owner.

Because of the breed's superior intelligence, the Standard Schnauzer is not the dog for everyone. They can be willfully strong-minded individuals, more than some owners can deal with. Standard Schnauzers constantly try new ways to test the limits with their owners. Sometimes it is amusing, and sometimes anything but amusing. Some Standard Schnauzers have an amazing sense of humor, while others are very serious about everything in their lives.

The Standard Schnauzer needs consistent firm leadership, but never by harsh or overbearing methods. The Standard Schnauzer will work readily and happily if praised for positive behavior; punishment for bad behavior never impresses the Standard Schnauzer. An owner must have the proverbial "patience of Job" and a strong iron will equal to that of the dog he is training. You must establish your authority as "pack leader" or the Standard Schnauzer will claim the title for himself.

The recommended ideal age to train a pup varies from trainer to

Versatile and agile, Standard Schnauzers can be trained to a high degree of excellence in competitive events. This is Ch. Pepper Tree Bel Air Austin CD, OA, OAJ, clearing the high jump in an agility trial.

trainer. Unfortunately, some trainers do not know how to work with very young puppies, leaving new owners to fend for themselves until their pup is six to eight months of age. This, I feel, is too late for the average owner of the Standard Schnauzer. I am a firm believer in starting the owner and his pup in gentle training as early as possible. The earlier you start, the more you can use the gentler training methods with great success.

Standard Schnauzers are very quick to pick up new commands if explained to them in a logical way. Never assume that, because the Schnauzer is so smart, you can skip a few steps in the learning process. However, once a command is learned, a Standard Schnauzer will never forget it. Of course, some clever Standard

Author and breeder Barbara Dille gives her friend Phlash a little pick-me-up.

Schnauzers will figure out variations or test their owners to make sure the command is a mandatory one. Trainers and owners must make sure that each command is taught properly the first time or else errors will haunt them forever, especially for an owner who plans to work in competition or performance events with his dog.

One very important note is that the breed on the whole will not tolerate excessive repetition like some other breeds do. Boredom is a word not in the Standard Schnauzer's vocabulary.

It's worth mentioning here that if you've adopted an adult dog that is completely trained to your liking, lucky you! You're off

A well-trained Standard Schnauzer like Simon is a joy to share your home with; whether or not you share your bed is up to you!

There's not much a Standard Schnauzer can't do! Although not a carting dog by nature, the breed is certainly capable of giving a friend a lift.

the hook! However, if that dog spent his life up to this point in a kennel, or even in a good home but without any real training, be prepared to tackle the job ahead. An adult dog with no previous training cannot be blamed for not knowing what he was never taught. While the dog is trying to understand and learn your rules, at the same time he has to unlearn many of his previously self-taught habits and general view of the world.

Working with a professional trainer will speed up your progress with an adopted adult dog. You'll need patience, too. Some new rules may be close to impossible for the dog to accept. After all, he's been successful so far by doing everything his way! (Patience again.) He may agree with your instruction for a few days and then slip back into his old ways, so you must be just as consistent and understanding in your teaching as you would be with a puppy. (More patience needed yet again!) Your dog has to learn to pay attention to your

OUR CANINE KIDS

"Everything I learned about parenting, I learned from my dog." How often adults recognize that their parenting skills are mere extensions of the education they acquired while caring for their dogs. Many owners refer to their dogs as their "kids" and treat their canine companions like real members of the family. Surveys indicate that a majority of dog owners talk to their dogs regularly, celebrate their dogs' birthdays and purchase Christmas gifts for their dogs. Another survey shows that dog owners take their dogs to the veterinarian more frequently than they visit their own physicians.

voice, your family, the daily routine, new smells, new sounds and, in some cases, even a new climate.

One of the most important things to find out about a newly adopted adult dog is his reaction to children (yours and others), strangers and your friends, and how he acts upon meeting other dogs. If he was not socialized with dogs as a puppy, this could be a major problem. This does not mean that he's a "bad" dog, a vicious dog or an aggressive dog; rather, it means that he has no idea how to read another dog's body language. There's no way for him to tell whether the other dog is a friend or foe. Survival instinct takes over, telling him to attack first and ask questions later. This definitely calls for professional help and, even then, may not be a behavior that can be corrected 100% reliably (or even at all). If you have a puppy, this is why it is so very important to introduce your young puppy properly to other puppies and "dog-friendly" adult dogs.

HOUSE-TRAINING YOUR STANDARD SCHNAUZER

Dogs are tactility-oriented when it comes to house-training. In other words, they respond to the surface on which they are given approval to eliminate. The choice is yours (the dog's version is in parentheses): The lawn (including the neighbors' lawns)? A bare patch of earth under a tree (where people like to sit and relax in the summertime)? Concrete steps or patio (all sidewalks, garages and basement floors)? The curbside (watch out for cars)? A small area of crushed stone in a corner of the yard (mine!)? The latter is the best choice if you can manage it, because it will remain strictly for

Puppies learn by watching their dam. Before your pup arrived at your home, he spent at least eight weeks observing his mother's manners and habits.

BASIC PRINCIPLES OF DOG TRAINING

1. Start training early. A young puppy is ready, willing and able.
2. Timing is your all-important tool. Praise at the exact time that the dog responds correctly. Pay close attention.
3. Patience is almost as important as timing!
4. Repeat! The same word has to mean the same thing every time.
5. In the beginning, praise all correct behavior verbally, along with treats and petting.

the dog's use and is easy to keep clean.

You can start out with paper-training indoors and switch over to an outdoor surface as the puppy matures and gains control over his need to eliminate. For the naysayers, don't worry—this won't mean that the dog will soil on every piece of newspaper lying around the house. You are training him to go outside, remember? Starting out by paper-training often is the only choice for a city dog.

WHEN YOUR PUPPY'S "GOT TO GO"
Your puppy's need to relieve himself is seemingly non-stop, but

What puppy doesn't appreciate a treat for a job well done?

signs of improvement will be seen each week. From 8–10 weeks old, the puppy will have to be taken outside every time he wakes up, about 10–15 minutes after every meal and after every period of play—all day long, from first thing in the morning until his bedtime! That's a total of ten or more trips per day to teach the puppy where it's okay to relieve himself. With that schedule in mind, you can see that house-training a young puppy is not a part-time job. It requires someone to be home all day.

If that seems overwhelming or impossible, do a little planning. For example, plan to pick up your puppy at the start of a vacation period. If you can't get home in the middle of the day, plan to hire a dog-sitter or ask a neighbor to come over to take the pup outside, feed him his lunch and then take him out again about ten or so minutes after he's eaten. Also make arrangements with that or another person to be your "emergency" contact if you have to stay late on the job. Remind yourself—repeatedly—that this hectic schedule improves as the puppy gets older.

HOME WITHIN A HOME
Your Standard Schnauzer puppy needs to be confined to one secure, puppy-proof area when no one is able to watch his every move. Generally the kitchen is the

CANINE DEVELOPMENT SCHEDULE

It is important to understand how and at what age a puppy develops into adulthood. If you are a puppy owner, consult the following Canine Development Schedule to determine the stage of development your puppy is currently experiencing. This knowledge will help you as you work with the puppy in the weeks and months ahead.

PERIOD	AGE	CHARACTERISTICS
FIRST TO THIRD	BIRTH TO SEVEN WEEKS	Puppy needs food, sleep and warmth and responds to simple and gentle touching. Needs mother for security and disciplining. Needs littermates for learning and interacting with other dogs. Pup learns to function within a pack and learns pack order of dominance. Begin socializing pup with adults and children for short periods. Pup begins to become aware of his environment.
FOURTH	EIGHT TO TWELVE WEEKS	Brain is fully developed. Pup needs socializing with outside world. Remove from mother and littermates. Needs to change from canine pack to human pack. Human dominance necessary. Fear period occurs between 8 and 12 weeks. Avoid fright and pain.
FIFTH	THIRTEEN TO SIXTEEN WEEKS	Training and formal obedience should begin. Less association with other dogs, more with people, places, situations. Period will pass easily if you remember this is pup's change-to-adolescence time. Be firm and fair. Flight instinct prominent. Permissiveness and over-disciplining can do permanent damage. Praise for good behavior.
JUVENILE	FOUR TO EIGHT MONTHS	Another fear period about 7 to 8 months of age. It passes quickly, but be cautious of fright and pain. Sexual maturity reached. Dominant traits established. Dog should understand sit, down, come and stay by now.

NOTE: THESE ARE APPROXIMATE TIME FRAMES. ALLOW FOR INDIVIDUAL DIFFERENCES IN PUPPIES.

POTTY COMMAND

Most dogs love to please their masters; there are no bounds to what dogs will do to make their owners happy. The potty command is a good example of this theory. If toileting on command makes the master happy, then more power to him. Puppies will obligingly piddle if it really makes their keepers smile. The Standard Schnauzer is a breed that takes very well to being trained to eliminate on command when started as a young pup. Some owners can be creative about which word they will use to command their dogs to relieve themselves. Some popular choices are "Potty," "Tinkle," "Piddle," "Let's go," "Hurry up" and "Toilet." Give the command every time your puppy goes into position and the puppy will begin to associate his business with the command.

place of choice because the floor is washable. Likewise, it's a busy family area that will accustom the pup to a variety of noises, everything from pots and pans to the telephone, blender and dishwasher. He will also be enchanted by the smell of your cooking (and will never be critical when you burn something). A sturdy exercise pen (also called an "ex-pen," a puppy version of a playpen), with high sides so that pup cannot climb out, within the puppy-proofed room can help confine a young pup. He can see out and has a certain amount of space in which to run about, but he is safe from dangerous things like electrical cords, heating units, trash baskets or open kitchen-supply cabinets. Place the pen where the puppy will not get a blast of heat or air conditioning.

In the pen, you can put a few toys, his bed (which can be his crate if the dimensions of pen and crate are compatible) and a few layers of newspaper in one small corner, just in case. A water bowl can be hung at a convenient height on the side of the ex-pen so it won't become a splashing pool for an innovative puppy. His food dish can go on the floor, next to but not under the water bowl.

Crates are something that pet owners are at last getting used to for their dogs. Wild or domestic canines have always preferred to sleep in den-like safe spots, and that is exactly what the crate provides. How often have you seen adult dogs that choose to sleep under a table or chair even though they have full run of the house? It's the den connection.

In your "happy" voice, use the word "Crate" every time you put the pup into his den. If he's new to a crate, toss in a small biscuit for him to chase the first few times. At night, after he's been outside, he should sleep in his crate. A good rule of thumb for the amount of time a pup can be in his crate during the day is one hour longer than the pup's age in months (e.g., four hours for a three-month-old puppy). Usually by four months of age, a puppy

Igor and Glenda demonstrate the joys of having a clean and well-behaved Standard Schnauzer for a companion.

can stay clean for seven to eight hours overnight in his crate.

The crate may be kept in his designated area at night or, if you want to be sure to hear those wake-up yips in the morning, put the crate in a corner of your bedroom. However, don't make any response whatsoever to whining or crying. If he's completely ignored, he'll settle down and get to sleep.

Good bedding for a young puppy is an old folded bath towel or an old blanket, something that is easily washable and disposable if necessary ("accidents" will happen!). Never put newspaper in the puppy's crate. Also, those old ideas about adding a clock to replace his mother's heartbeat, or a hot-water bottle to replace her warmth, are just that—old ideas. The clock could drive the puppy nuts, and the hot-water bottle could end up as a very soggy waterbed! An extremely good breeder would have introduced

DAILY SCHEDULE

How many relief trips does your puppy need per day? A puppy up to the age of 14 weeks will need to go outside about 8 to 12 times per day! You will have to take the pup out any time he starts sniffing around the floor or turning in small circles, as well as after naps, meals, games and lessons or whenever he's released from his crate. Once the puppy is 14 to 22 weeks of age, he will require only 6 to 8 relief trips. At the ages of 22 to 32 weeks, the puppy will require about 5 to 7 trips. Adult dogs typically require 4 relief trips per day, in the morning, afternoon, evening and late at night.

TIDY BOY

Clean by nature, dogs do not like to soil their dens, which in effect are their crates or sleeping quarters. Unless not feeling well, dogs will not defecate or urinate in their crates. Crate training capitalizes on the dog's natural desire to keep his den clean. Be conscientious about giving the puppy as many opportunities to relieve himself outdoors as possible. Reward the puppy for correct behavior. Praise him and pat him whenever he "goes" in the correct location. Even the tidiest of puppies can have potty accidents, so be patient and dedicate more energy to helping your puppy achieve a clean lifestyle.

your puppy to the crate by letting two pups sleep together for a couple of nights, followed by several nights alone. How thankful you will be if you found that breeder!

Safe toys in the pup's crate or area will keep him occupied, but monitor their condition closely. Discard any toys that show signs of being chewed to bits. Squeaky parts, bits of stuffing or plastic or any other small pieces can cause intestinal blockage or possibly choking if swallowed.

PROGRESSING WITH POTTY-TRAINING
After you've taken your puppy out and he has relieved himself in the area you've selected, he can have some free time with the family as long as there is someone responsible for watching him. That doesn't mean just someone in the same room who is watching TV or busy on the computer, but one person who is doing nothing other than keeping an eye on the pup, playing with him on the floor and helping him understand his position in the pack.

This first taste of freedom will let you begin to set the house rules. If you don't want the dog on the furniture, now is the time to prevent his first attempts to jump up onto the couch. The word to use in this case is "Off," not "Down." "Down" is the word you will use to teach the down position, which is something entirely different.

EXTRA! EXTRA!
The headlines read: "Puppy Piddles Here!" Breeders commonly use newspapers to line their whelping pens, so puppies learn to associate newspapers with relieving themselves. Do not use newspapers to line your pup's crate, as this will signal to your puppy that it is OK to urinate in his crate. If you choose to paper-train your puppy, you will layer newspapers on a section of the floor near the door he uses to go outside. You should encourage the puppy to use the papers to relieve himself, and bring him there whenever you see him getting ready to go. Little by little, you will reduce the size of the newspaper-covered area so that the puppy will learn to relieve himself "on the other side of the door."

Most corrections at this stage come in the form of simply distracting the puppy. Instead of telling him "No" for "Don't chew the carpet," distract the chomping puppy with a toy and he'll forget about the carpet.

As you are playing with the pup, do not forget to watch him closely and pay attention to his body language. Whenever you see him begin to circle or sniff, take the puppy outside to relieve himself. If you are paper-training, put him back into his confined area on the newspapers. In either case, praise him as he eliminates while he actually is *in the act* of relieving himself. Three seconds after he has finished is too late! You'll be praising him for running toward you, picking up a toy or whatever he may be doing at that moment, and that's not what you want to be praising him for. Timing is a vital tool in all dog training. Use it!

Remove soiled newspapers immediately and replace them with clean ones. You may want to take a small piece of soiled paper and place it in the middle of the new clean papers, as the scent will attract him to that spot when it's time to go again. That scent attraction is why it's so important to clean up any messes made in the house by using a product specially made to eliminate the odor of dog urine and droppings. Regular household cleansers won't do the trick. Pet shops sell the best pet deodorizers. Invest in the largest container you can find.

Scent attraction eventually will lead your pup to his chosen spot outdoors if you have a fenced yard; this is the basis of outdoor training. When you take your puppy outside to relieve himself, use a one-word command such as "Outside" or "Go-potty" (that's one word to the puppy!) as you pick him up and attach his leash. Then put him down in his area. If for any reason you can't carry him, snap the leash on quickly and lead him to his spot. Now comes the hard part—hard for you, that is. Just stand there until he urinates and defecates. Move him a few feet in one direction or another if he's just sitting there looking at you, but remember that this is neither playtime nor time for a walk. This is strictly a business trip! Then, as he circles and squats (remember your timing!), give him a quiet "Good dog" as praise. If you start to jump for joy, ecstatic over his perform- ance, he'll do one of two things: either he will stop mid-stream, as it were, or he'll do it again for you—in the house—and expect you to be just as delighted!

Give him five minutes or so and, if he doesn't go in that time, take him back indoors to his confined area and try again in another ten minutes, or immedi- ately if you see him sniffing and

The nose knows where to go! Dogs of all ages use their sense of scent to find a pleasing relief spot.

SOMEBODY TO BLAME

House-training a puppy can be frustrating for the puppy and the owner alike. The puppy does not instinctively understand the difference between defecating on the pavement outside and on the ceramic tile in the kitchen. He is confused and frightened by his human's exuberant reactions to his natural urges. The owner, arguably the more intelligent of the duo, is also frustrated that he cannot convince his puppy to obey his commands and instructions.

In frustration, the owner may struggle with the temptation to discipline the puppy, scold him or even strike him on the rear end. Harsh corrections are unnecessary and inappropriate, serving to defeat your purpose in gaining your puppy's trust and respect. Don't blame your nine-week-old puppy. Blame yourself for not being 100% consistent in the puppy's lessons and routine. The lesson here is simple: try harder and your puppy will succeed.

circling. By careful observation, you'll soon work out a successful schedule.

Accidents, by the way, are just that—accidents. Clean them up quickly and thoroughly, without comment, after the puppy has been taken outside to finish his business and then put back into his area or crate. If you witness an accident in progress, say "No!" in a stern voice and get the pup outdoors immediately. No punishment is needed. You and your puppy are just learning each other's language, and sometimes it's easy to miss a puppy's message. Chalk it up to experience and watch more closely from now on.

KEEPING THE PACK ORDERLY
Discipline is a form of training that brings order to life. For example, military discipline is what allows the soldiers in an army to work as one. Discipline is a form of teaching and, in dogs, is the basis of how the successful pack operates. Each member knows his place in the pack and all respect the leader, or Alpha dog. It is essential for your puppy that you establish this type of relationship, with you as the Alpha, or leader. It is a form of social coexistence that all canines recognize and accept. Discipline, therefore, is never to be confused with punishment. When you teach your puppy how you want him to behave, and he behaves properly and you praise him for it, you are disciplining him with a form of positive reinforcement.

For a dog, rewards come in the form of praise, a smile, a cheerful tone of voice, a few friendly pats or a rub of the ears. Rewards are also small food treats. Obviously, that does not mean bits of regular dog food. Instead, treats are very small bits of special things like cheese or pieces of soft dog treats. The idea is to reward the dog with something very small that he can taste and swallow, providing instant positive reinforcement. If he has to take time to chew the treat, by the time he is finished he will have forgotten what he did to earn it!

Your puppy should never be physically punished. The displeasure shown on your face and in your voice is sufficient to signal to the pup that he has done something wrong. He wants to please everyone higher up on the social ladder, especially his leader, so a scowl and harsh

WHO'S TRAINING WHOM?
Dog training is a black-and-white exercise. The correct response to a command must be absolute, and the trainer must insist on completely accurate responses from the dog. A trainer cannot command his dog to sit and then settle for the dog's melting into the down position. Often owners are so pleased that their dogs "did something" in response to a command that they just shrug and say, "OK, down" even though they wanted the dog to sit. You want your dog to respond to the command without hesitation: he must respond at that moment and correctly every time.

voice will take care of the error. Growling out the word "Shame!" when the pup is caught in the act of doing something wrong is better than the repetitive "No." Some dogs hear "No" so often that they begin to think it's their name! By the way, do not use the dog's name when you're correcting him. His name is reserved to get his attention for something pleasant about to take place.

There are punishments that have nothing to do with you. For example, your dog may think that chasing cats is one reason for his existence. You can try to stop it as much as you like but without success, because it's such fun for the dog. But one good hissing, spitting swipe of a cat's claws across the dog's nose will put an end to the game forever. Intervene only when your dog's eyeball is seriously at risk. Cat scratches can cause permanent damage to an innocent but annoying puppy.

The most important ingredient in your training program is praise, and plenty of it.

PUPPY KINDERGARTEN

COLLAR AND LEASH

Before you begin your Standard Schnauzer puppy's education, he must be used to his collar and leash. Choose a collar for your puppy that is secure, but not heavy or bulky. He won't enjoy training if he's uncomfortable. A flat buckle collar is fine for everyday wear and for initial puppy training. For older dogs, there are several types of training collars such as the martingale, which is a double loop that tightens slightly around the neck, or the head collar, which is similar to a horse's halter. Do not use any type of training collar unless you have been specifically shown how to put it on and how to use it. Your breeder or a good trainer can advise you about the different types of training collars.

A lightweight 6-foot woven cotton or leather training leash is preferred by most trainers because it is easy to fold up in your hand and comfortable to hold because there is a certain amount of give to it. There are lessons where the dog will start off 6 feet away from you at the end of the leash. The leash used to take the puppy outside to relieve himself is shorter because you don't want him to roam away from his area. The shorter leash will also be the one to use when you walk the puppy.

If you've been wise enough to enroll in a puppy kindergarten training class, suggestions will be made as to the best collar and leash for your young puppy. I say "wise" because your puppy will be in a class with puppies in his age range (up to five months old) of all breeds and sizes. It's the perfect way for him to learn the right way (and the wrong way) to interact with other dogs as well as their people. You cannot teach your puppy how to interpret another dog's sign language. For a first-time puppy owner, these socialization classes are invaluable. For experienced dog owners, they are a real boon to further training.

ATTENTION

You've been using the dog's name since the minute you collected him from the breeder, so you should be able to get his attention by saying his name—with a big smile and in an excited tone of voice. His response will be the puppy equivalent of "Here I am! What are we going to do?" Your immediate response (if you haven't guessed by now) is "Good dog." Rewarding him at the moment he pays attention to you teaches him the proper way to respond when he hears his name.

EXERCISES FOR A BASIC CANINE EDUCATION

THE SIT EXERCISE

There are several ways to teach the puppy to sit. The first one is to catch him whenever he is about to sit and, as his backside nears the floor, say "Sit, good dog!" That's positive reinforcement and, if your timing is sharp, he will learn that what he's doing at that second is connected to your saying "Sit" and that you think he's clever for doing it!

Another method is to start with the puppy on his leash in front of you. Show him a treat in the palm of your right hand. Bring your hand up under his nose and, almost in slow motion, move your hand up and back so his nose goes up in the air and his head tilts back as he follows the treat in your hand. At that point, he will have to either sit or fall over, so as his back legs buckle under, say "Sit, good dog," and then give him the treat

You won't get very far with your lesson if the dog is distracted and not focusing his attention on you.

and lots of praise. You may have to begin with your hand lightly running up his chest, actually lifting his chin up until he sits. Some (usually older) dogs require gentle pressure on their hindquarters with the left hand, in which case the dog should be on your left side. Puppies generally do not appreciate this physical dominance.

After a few times, you should be able to show the dog a treat in the open palm of your hand, raise your hand waist-high as you say "Sit" and have him sit. You thereby will have taught him two things at the same time; both the verbal command and the motion

Sitting at attention and looking up at his leader, Vortac Phlying Tiger is ready to learn something new.

of the hand are signals for the sit. Your puppy is watching you almost more than he is listening to you, so what you do is just as important as what you say.

Don't save any of these drills only for training sessions. Use them as much as possible at odd times during a normal day. The dog should always sit before being given his food dish. He should sit to let you go through a doorway first, when the doorbell rings or when you stop to speak to someone on the street.

THE DOWN EXERCISE

Before beginning to teach the down command, you must consider how the dog feels about this exercise. To him, "down" is a submissive position. Being flat on the floor with you standing over him is not his idea of fun. It's up to you to let him know that, while it may not be fun, the reward of your approval is worth his effort.

Start with the puppy on your left side in a sit position. Hold the leash right above his collar in your left hand. Have an extra-special treat, such as a small piece of cooked chicken or hot dog, in your right hand. Place it at the end of the pup's nose and steadily move your hand down and forward along the ground, between the pup's front paws. Do not move the food forward more than two inches in front of his paws. Hold the leash to prevent a sudden lunge for the food. As the puppy goes into the down position, say "Down" very gently.

The difficulty with this exercise is twofold: it's both the submissive aspect and the fact that most people say the word "Down" as if they were drill sergeants in charge of recruits! So issue the command sweetly, give him the treat and have the pup maintain the down position for several seconds. If he tries to get up immediately, place your hands on his shoulders and press down gently, giving him a very quiet "Good dog." As you progress with this lesson, increase the "down time" until he will hold it until you say "Okay" (his cue for release). Practice this one in the house at various times throughout the day.

By increasing the length of time during which the dog must maintain the down position, you'll find many uses for it. For example, he can lie at your feet in the vet's office or anywhere that both of you have to wait, when you are on the phone, while the family is eating and so forth. If you progress to training for competitive obedience, he'll already be all set for the exercise called the "long down."

THE STAY EXERCISE

You can teach your Standard Schnauzer to stay in the sit, down and stand positions. To teach the

sit/stay, have the dog sit on your left side. Hold the leash at waist level in your left hand and let the dog know that you have a treat in your closed right hand. Step forward on your right foot as you say "Stay." Immediately turn and stand directly in front of the dog, keeping your right hand up high so he'll keep his eye on the treat hand and maintain the sit position for a count of five. Return to your original position and offer the reward.

Increase the length of the sit/stay each time until the dog can hold it for at least 30 seconds without moving. After about a week of success, move out on your right foot and take two steps before turning to face the dog. Give the "Stay" hand signal (left palm held up, facing the dog) as you leave. He gets the treat when you return and he holds the sit/stay. Increase the distance that

A gentle approach and a tasty reward will help coax your Standard Schnauzer into the down position.

you walk away from him before turning until you reach the length of your training leash. But don't rush it! Go back to the beginning if he moves before he should. No matter what the lesson, never be upset by having to back up for a few days. The repetition and practice are what will make your dog reliable in these commands. It won't do any good to move on to something more difficult if the command is not mastered at the easier levels. Above all, even if you do get frustrated, never let your puppy know! Always keep a positive, upbeat attitude during training, which will transmit to your dog for positive results.

The down/stay is taught in the same way once the dog is completely reliable and steady with the down command. Again, don't rush it. With the dog in the down position on your left side, step out on your right foot as you say "Stay." Return by walking around in back of the dog and into your original position. While you are training, it's okay to murmur something like "Hold on" to encourage him to stay put. When the dog will stay without moving when you are at a distance of 3 or 4 feet, begin to increase the length of time before you return. Be sure he holds the down on your return until you say "Okay." At that point, he gets his treat—just so he'll remember for next time that it's not over until it's over.

THE COME EXERCISE

Probably one of the hardest yet most important commands to ensure that your Standard Schnauzer responds to absolutely reliably is "Come." This is especially true when there is a squirrel or other small, fast, scurrying-type animal in the Standard Schnauzer's line of sight. The Standard Schnauzer's inherited ratting instinct is extremely strong in some individuals, thus "running interference" in your lesson plans. If you make teaching "Come" a positive experience, you encourage a reliable response, which is necessary for your dog's safety.

In fact, no command is more important to the safety of your Standard Schnauzer than "Come." It is what you should say every single time you see the puppy running toward you: "Binky, come! Good dog." During playtime, run a few feet away

With the pup on a training leash, increase the distance that you move away from him as he stays.

Once your dog is comfortable with the down exercise, you can progress to the down/stay.

from the puppy and turn and tell him to "Come" as he is already running to you.

Teaching this command can be started as a game within a day or two of bringing your pup home. Done correctly and consistently, this game will bring your dog running to you in spite of distractions for his entire life. To begin, have all members of the family, even the young children, participate in this game. Have each person take a few small yummy treats and go to a different corner of the room. You should not use crunchy treats but rather ones that

are easy to chew, such as bits of cheese or soft training treats broken into pieces. Everyone takes turns calling the puppy's name followed by the word "Come" in a cheerful tone of voice. Keep using the happy and excited voice to praise the pup as he comes to you, and reward the pup with a treat and petting as he arrives at your feet.

Do this exercise for no longer than a couple of minutes at any one time, several times a day. After a few days, each person can take his treats and go somewhere that is out of the pup's sight, such

With arms outstretched and a happy voice, make coming to you something that your Standard Schnauzer always looks forward to.

as behind a piece of furniture or to another room. Remember how important this command is for your puppy to learn and make sure that everyone is on the same page when it comes to being consistent in teaching him. Anytime anyone calls the dog for the next few weeks, he must have a treat handy. When the pup is responding quickly and reliably every time, start randomizing the treats, but never stop the praise.

Next, try the command with the puppy on the training leash. This time, catch him off guard, while he's sniffing a leaf or watching a bird: "Binky, come!" You may have to pause for a split second after his name to be sure you have his attention. If the puppy shows any sign of confusion, give the leash a mild jerk and take a couple of steps backward to encourage him to come to you. Do not repeat the command. In this case, you should say "Good come" as he reaches you.

An important rule of training is that each command word is given just once. Anything more is nagging. You'll also notice that all commands are one word only. Even when they are actually two words, you say them as one.

It is very important to remember to never call the dog to you to scold him. Put yourself·in the dog's position: would you want to go to someone if you were going to be punished? Your dog must always connect "Come" with something pleasant and with your approval; that way you can rely on his response.

Puppies, like children, have notoriously short attention spans, so don't overdo it with any of the training. Keep each lesson short. Break it up with a quick run around the yard or a ball toss, repeat the lesson and quit as soon as the pup gets it right. That way, you will always end with a "Good dog."

OKAY!

This is the signal that tells your dog that he can quit whatever he was doing. Use "Okay" to end a session on a correct response to a command. (Never end on an incorrect response.) Lots of praise follows. People use "Okay" a lot and it has other uses for dogs, too. Your dog is barking. You say, "Okay! Come!" "Okay" signals him to stop the barking activity and "Come" allows him to come to you for a "Good dog."

THE HEEL EXERCISE

Before you can teach the puppy to heel, you must teach the dog who exactly is the leader of the walk and that walking is much more comfortable for both of you on a loose lead (rather than a tight one from his pulling ahead or lagging behind). Have the puppy on your left side and with the command "Let's go," start off on your left foot. Keep up a running happy conversation with the puppy. If the pup bolts ahead of you, stop abruptly and reverse your direction while continuing to talk happily to the pup. When the dog is by your side, give him a tasty morsel with your left hand. After doing this a few times, you will find that you have a pup that is happily walking by your side on a loose lead.

Once you've mastered on-leash walking, your pup is ready to learn the heel command. For the heel command, the dog must give you his full attention while remaining extremely close to, but not touching, your left leg. When you come to a halt, the dog will eventually automatically sit.

Start off with the dog sitting by your left side. Give your dog the command of his name and the word "Heel." Proceed approximately 6 feet and halt. Have a piece of food in your left hand and slowly bring the food up above the dog's head, which will make the dog sit. Give lavish praise along with the tidbit. Repeat this process two or three more times. Gradually, over a period of days, increase the length of time that you keep the dog in the heel position. Always remember to release the pup with a command such as "Okay," "All done" or "OK, good dog." Intersperse the heel command with the less formal "Let's go" command, allowing the dog the

While your focus is on positive reinforcement, your dog may need a verbal scolding from time to time. It doesn't take more than a few disapproving words to get your point across.

freedom to relieve himself and just plain sniff around but not allowing him to pull you.

LET'S GO!

Many people use "Let's go" instead of "Heel" when teaching their dogs to behave on lead. It sounds more like fun! When beginning to teach the heel, whatever command you use, always step off on your left foot. That's the one next to the dog, who is on your left side, in case you've forgotten. Keep a loose leash. When the dog pulls ahead, stop, bring him back and begin again. Use treats to guide him around turns.

TAPERING OFF TIDBITS

Your dog has been watching you—and the hand that treats— throughout all of his lessons, and now it's time to break the treat habit. Begin by giving him treats at the end of each lesson only. Then start to give a treat after the end of only some of the lessons. At the end of every lesson, as well as during the lessons, be consistent with the praise. Your pup now doesn't know whether he'll get a treat or not, but he should keep performing well just in case! Finally, you will stop giving treat rewards entirely. Save them for something brand-new that you want to teach him. Keep up the praise and you'll always have a "good dog."

OBEDIENCE CLASSES

It is recommended that every owner enroll his puppy in an obedience class. Many training clubs and training schools accept puppies as young as three months old in puppy kinder-garten classes. Many areas have dog clubs that offer not only the basic obedience classes and Canine Good Citizen® (CGC) preparation classes but also classes to prepare owners and dogs for competition in obedience, agility, rally obedience and more. Some even offer training for freestyle (a competitive event described as "dancing with dogs").

If you prefer one-on-one training for you and your pup, ask your veterinarian or breeder for recommendations. You can also go online and find trainers in your area by searching the sites of two national dog-trainer organizations: the National Association of Dog Obedience Instructors (www.nadoi.org) and the Association of Pet Dog Trainers (www.apdt.org). Whatever you do, it is recommended that you start training as soon as possible with your puppy, as the Standard Schnauzer is a very intelligent dog, a breed that needs a job to do. A professional trainer will help guide you in the right direction. Your dog will learn new behaviors, but, just as importantly, you will learn how to teach your dog so that the dog does what you want him to do, not the other way around!

OTHER ACTIVITIES FOR LIFE

The Standard Schnauzer is, mentally and physically, probably one of the most versatile breeds of dog. Most Standard Schnauzers are very well suited to participating in most any dog sport or type of work that a person can dream up. The Standard Schnauzer's amazing attention to detail, very determined mind and never-ending curiosity have made the breed successful as hearing dogs

TIPS FOR TRAINING AND SAFETY

1. Whether on or off leash, practice only in a fenced area.
2. Remove the training collar when the training session is over.
3. Don't try to break up a dogfight.
4. "Come," "Leave it" and "Wait" are safety commands.
5. The dog belongs in a crate or behind a barrier when riding in the car.
6. Don't ignore the dog's first sign of aggression. Aggression only gets worse, so take it seriously.
7. Keep the faces of children and dogs separated.
8. Pay attention to what the dog is chewing.
9. Keep the vet's number near your phone.
10. "Okay" is a useful release command.

for the deaf, assistance dogs for the handicapped, therapy dogs in critical-care hospitals and nursing homes, police workers, search-and-rescue (SAR) dogs, melanoma cancer-detection dogs and even retrievers of birds in the field. You name it and a Standard Schnauzer has done it...or is doing it.

tors is the high maintenance required for the breed's coat, making year-round competition doubly time-consuming. The handler needs time for both training and grooming.

Nevertheless, Standard Schnauzers participate with devotees of our breed in many formal and informal dog sports, such as obedience, tracking, agility, flyball and, more recently, herding and lure coursing, to name a few. With his strongly muscled, square, compact body, combined with an extraordinary degree of canine intelligence, this is truly a most versatile companion animal.

Some Standard Schnauzer owners also have the opportunity to participate in the classic German training/competition program known as Schutzhund, although this is more commonly pursued by the Standard Schnauzer's "Giant" cousin. Although originally bred as ratters, Standard Schnauzers make excellent watchdogs, and their high degree of intelligence

Although an area of competition traditionally for sighthounds, lure coursing is not beyond the scope or stride of the Standard Schnauzer.

The breed certainly does hold its own in formal competition when trained by a good owner/trainer. Probably the reason that the Standard Schnauzer is not one of the more popular canine competi-

Tracking trials are popular events in which Standard Schnauzers apply their sensational noses to find articles laid on a track.

Standard Schnauzers naturally adapt to the demands of herding trials, as this talented California dog illustrates with great panache in these three photos.

recommends them for these specialized tests.

Schutzhund originated as a test to determine the best quality working/protection dogs to be used for breeding stock. Breeders on the Continent and in the US continue to use it as a way to evaluate working ability and temperament. There are three levels in Schutzhund trials: SchH I, SchH II and SchH III, with each level being progressively more difficult to complete successfully. Each level consists of training, obedience and protection phases. Training for Schutzhund is intense and must be practiced consistently to keep the dog keen. The experience of Schutzhund training is rewarding for dog and owner, and the Standard Schnauzer is well suited to this type of training.

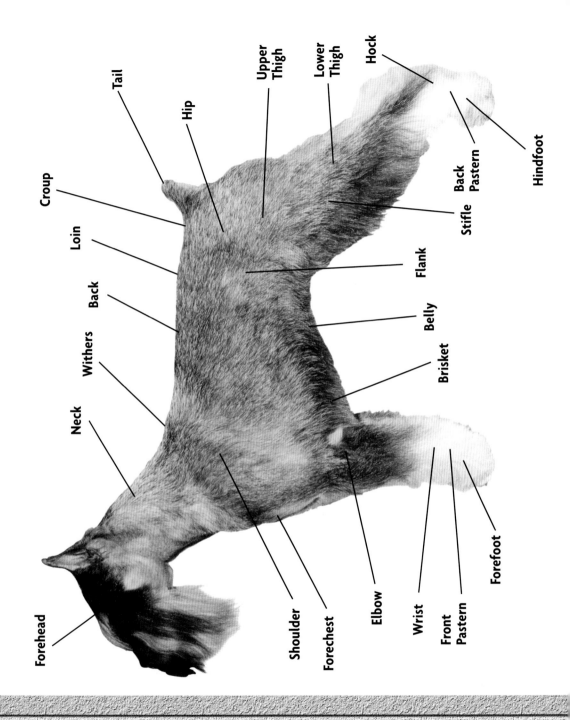

Tail

Hip

Upper
Thigh

Lower
Thigh

Hock

Croup

Back
Pastern

Hindfoot

Loin

Stifle

Back

Flank

Withers

Belly

Neck

Brisket

Forehead

Shoulder

Forechest

Elbow

Wrist

Front
Pastern

Forefoot

PHYSICAL STRUCTURE OF THE STANDARD SCHNAUZER

STANDARD SCHNAUZER

By Lowell Ackerman DVM, DACVD

HEALTHCARE FOR A LIFETIME

When you own a dog, you become his healthcare advocate over his entire lifespan, as well as being the one to shoulder the financial burden of such care. Accordingly, it is worthwhile to focus on prevention rather than treatment, as you and your pet will both be happier.

Of course, the best place to have begun your program of preventive healthcare is with the initial purchase or adoption of your dog. There is no way of guaranteeing that your new furry friend is free of medical problems, but there are some things you can do to improve your odds. You certainly should have done adequate research into the Standard Schnauzer and have selected your puppy carefully rather than buying on impulse. Health issues aside, a large number of pet abandonment and relinquishment cases arise from a mismatch between pet needs and owner expectations. This is entirely preventable with appropriate planning and finding a good breeder.

Regarding healthcare issues specifically, it is very difficult to make blanket statements about where to acquire a problem-free pet, but, again, a reputable breeder is your best bet. In an ideal situation you have the opportunity to see both parents, get references from other owners of the breeder's pups and see genetic-testing documentation for several generations of the litter's ancestors. At the very least, you must thoroughly investigate your Standard Schnauzer and the problems inherent in that breed, as well as the genetic testing available to screen for those problems. Genetic testing offers some important benefits but is available for only a few disorders in a relatively small number of breeds and is not available for some of the most common genetic diseases, such as hip dysplasia, cataracts, epilepsy, cardiomy-opathy, etc. This area of research is indeed exciting and increasingly important, and advances will continue to be made each year. In fact, recent research has shown that there is an equivalent dog gene for 75% of known human genes, so research done in either species is likely to benefit the other.

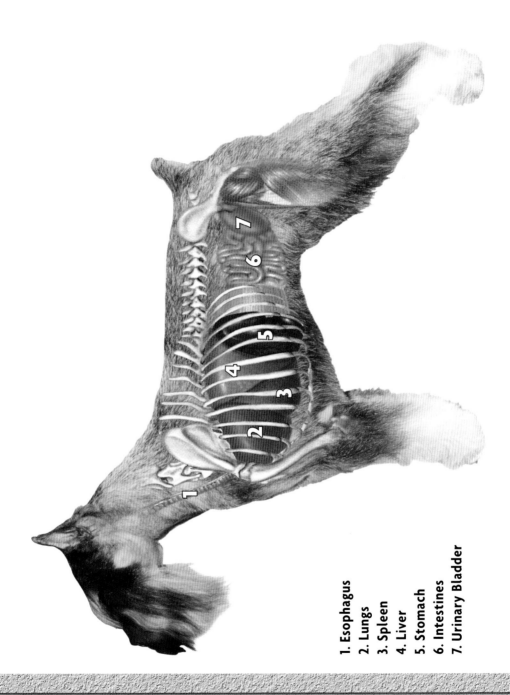

1. Esophagus
2. Lungs
3. Spleen
4. Liver
5. Stomach
6. Intestines
7. Urinary Bladder

INTERNAL ORGANS OF THE STANDARD SCHNAUZER

We've also discussed that evaluating the behavioral nature of your Standard Schnauzer and that of his immediate family members is an important part of the selection process that cannot be underestimated or overemphasized. It is sometimes difficult to evaluate temperament in puppies because certain behavioral tendencies, such as some forms of aggression, may not be immediately evident. More dogs are euthanized each year for behavioral reasons than for all medical conditions combined, so it is critical to take temperament issues seriously. Start with a well-balanced, friendly companion and put the time and effort into proper socialization, and you will both be greatly rewarded with a valued relationship.

Assuming that you have started off with a pup from healthy, sound stock, you then become responsible for helping your veterinarian keep your pet healthy. Some crucial things happen before you even bring your puppy home. Parasite control typically begins at two weeks of age, and vaccinations typically begin at six to eight weeks of age. A pre-pubertal evaluation is typically scheduled for about six months of age. At this time, a dental evaluation is done (since the adult teeth are now in), heartworm prevention is started and neutering or spaying is most commonly done.

It is critical to commence

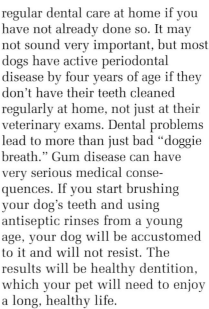

DENTAL WARNING SIGNS
A veterinary dental exam is necessary if you notice one or any combination of the following in your dog:
• Broken, loose or missing teeth
• Loss of appetite (which could be due to mouth pain or illness caused by infection)
• Gum abnormalities, including redness, swelling and bleeding
• Drooling, with or without blood
• Yellowing of the teeth or gumline, indicating tartar
• Bad breath

regular dental care at home if you have not already done so. It may not sound very important, but most dogs have active periodontal disease by four years of age if they don't have their teeth cleaned regularly at home, not just at their veterinary exams. Dental problems lead to more than just bad "doggie breath." Gum disease can have very serious medical consequences. If you start brushing your dog's teeth and using antiseptic rinses from a young age, your dog will be accustomed to it and will not resist. The results will be healthy dentition, which your pet will need to enjoy a long, healthy life.

Standard Schnauzers are physically mature around 18 months to 2 years of age (although they reach their "show prime" between 3 and 5 years old). Even

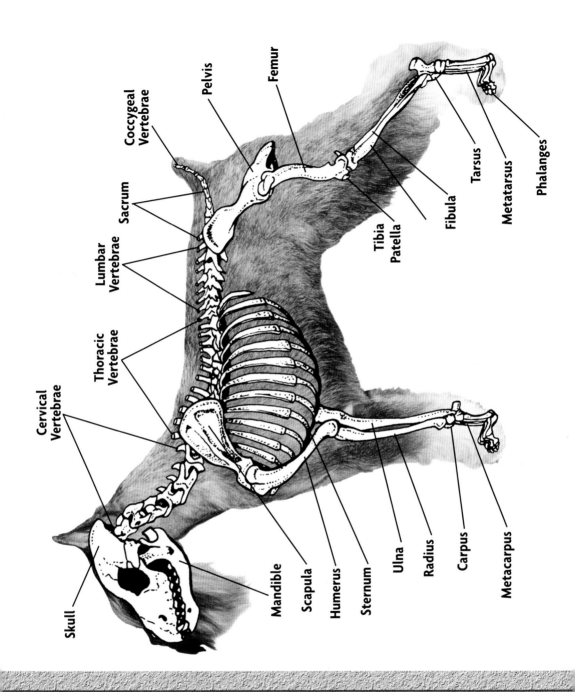

Coccygeal Vertebrae
Pelvis
Femur
Sacrum
Tibia
Patella
Fibula
Tarsus
Metatarsus
Phalanges
Lumbar Vertebrae
Thoracic Vertebrae
Cervical Vertebrae
Skull
Mandible
Scapula
Humerus
Sternum
Ulna
Radius
Carpus
Metacarpus

SKELETAL STRUCTURE OF THE STANDARD SCHNAUZER

individual dogs within each breed have different healthcare requirements, so work with your veterinarian to determine what will be needed and what your role should be. This doctor-client relationship is important, because as vaccination guidelines change, there may not be an annual "vaccine visit" scheduled. You must make sure that you see your veterinarian at least annually, even if no vaccines are due, because this is the best opportunity to coordinate healthcare activities and to make sure that no medical issues creep by unaddressed.

As your Standard Schnauzer advances in years, the vet will determine when to consider him a "senior" for healthcare purposes and will start him on a preventive senior-care routine. In general, if you've been taking great care of your canine companion throughout his formative and adult years, the transition to senior status should be a smooth one. Age is not a disease, and as long as everything is functioning as it should, there is no reason why most of late adulthood should not be rewarding for both you and your pet. This is especially true if you have tended to the details, such as regular veterinary visits, proper dental care, excellent nutrition and management of bone and joint issues.

SELECTING A VETERINARIAN

There is probably no more important decision that you will make regarding your pet's healthcare than the selection of his doctor. Your pet's veterinarian will be a pediatrician, family-practice physician and gerontologist, depending on the dog's life stage, and will be the individual who makes recommendations regarding issues such as when specialists

---

TAKING YOUR DOG'S TEMPERATURE

It is important to know how to take your dog's temperature at times when you think he may be ill. It's not the most enjoyable task, but it can be done without too much difficulty. It's easier with a helper, preferably someone with whom the dog is friendly, so that one of you can hold the dog while the other inserts the thermometer.

Before inserting the thermometer, coat the end with petroleum jelly. Insert the thermometer slowly and gently into the dog's rectum about one inch. Wait for the reading, about two minutes. Be sure to remove the thermometer carefully and clean it thoroughly after each use.

A dog's normal body temperature is between 100.5 and 102.5 degrees F. Immediate veterinary attention is required if the dog's temperature is below 99 or above 104 degrees F.

need to be consulted, when diagnostic testing and/or therapeutic intervention is needed and when you will need to seek outside emergency and critical-care services. Your vet will act as your advocate and liaison throughout these processes.

Everyone has his own idea about what to look for in a vet, an individual who will play a big role in his dog's (and, of course, his own) life for many years to come. For some, it is the compassionate caregiver with whom they hope to develop a professional relationship to span the lives of their dogs and even their future pets. For others, they are seeking a clinician with keen diagnostic and therapeutic insight who can deliver state-of-the-art healthcare. Still others need a veterinary facility that is open evenings and weekends, is in close proximity or provides mobile veterinary services to accommodate their schedules; these people may not much mind that their dogs might see different veterinarians on each visit. Just as we have different reasons for selecting our own healthcare professionals (e.g., covered by insurance plan, expert in field, convenient location, etc.), we should not expect that there is a one-size-fits-all recommendation

---

YOUR DOG NEEDS TO VISIT THE VET IF:
- He has ingested a toxin such as antifreeze or a toxic plant; in these cases, administer first aid and call the vet right away
- His teeth are discolored, loose or missing or he has sores or other signs of infection or abnormality in the mouth
- He has been vomiting, has had diarrhea or has been constipated for over 24 hours; call immediately if you notice blood
- He has refused food for over 24 hours
- His eating habits, water intake or toilet habits have noticeably changed; if you have noticed weight gain or weight loss
- He shows symptoms of bloat, which requires *immediate* attention
- He is salivating excessively
  - He has a lump in his throat
  - He has a lump or bumps anywhere on the body
  - He is very lethargic
  - He appears to be in pain or otherwise has trouble chewing or swallowing
  - His skin loses elasticity.
    Of course, there will be other instances in which a visit to the vet is necessary; these are just some of the signs that could be indicative of serious problems that need to be caught as early as possible.

for selecting a veterinarian and veterinary practice. The best advice is to be honest in your assessment of what you expect from a veterinary practice and to conscientiously research the options in your area. You will quickly appreciate that not all veterinary practices are the same, and you will be happiest with one that truly meets your needs.

There is another point to be considered in the selection of veterinary services. Not that long ago, a single veterinarian would attempt to manage all medical and surgical issues as they arose. That was often problematic, because veterinarians are trained in many species and many diseases, and it was just impossible for general veterinary practitioners to be experts in every species, breed, field and ailment. However, just as in the human healthcare fields, specialization has allowed general practitioners to concentrate on primary healthcare delivery, especially wellness and the prevention of infectious diseases, and to utilize a network of specialists to assist in the management of conditions that require specific expertise and experience. Thus there are now many types of veterinary specialists, including dermatologists, cardiologists, ophthalmologists, surgeons, internists, oncologists, neurologists, behaviorists, criticalists and others to help primary-care veteri-

A gleaming coat, fit body and alert demeanor all point to overall good health inside and out.

narians deal with complicated medical challenges. In most cases, specialists see cases referred by primary-care veterinarians, make diagnoses and set up management plans. From there, the animals' ongoing care is returned to their primary-care veterinarians. This important team approach to your pet's medical-care needs has provided opportunities for advanced care and an unparalleled level of quality to be delivered.

With all of the opportunities for your Standard Schnauzer to receive high-quality veterinary medical care, there is another topic that needs to be addressed at the same time—cost. It's been said that you can have excellent healthcare or inexpensive healthcare, but never both; this is as true in veterinary medicine as it is in human medicine. While veterinary costs are a fraction of what the same services cost in the human health-care arena, it is still difficult to deal with unanticipated medical costs, especially since they can easily creep into hundreds or even thousands of dollars if specialists or emergency services become involved. However, there are ways of managing these risks. The easiest is to buy pet health insurance and realize that its foremost purpose is not to cover routine healthcare visits but rather to serve as an umbrella for those rainy days when your pet needs medical care and you don't want to worry about whether or not you can afford that care.

Pet insurance policies are very cost-effective (and very inexpensive by human health-insurance standards), but make sure that you buy the policy long before you intend to use it (preferably starting in puppyhood, because coverage will exclude pre-existing conditions) and that you are actually buying an indemnity insurance plan from an insurance company that is regulated by your state or province. Many insurance policy look-alikes are actually discount clubs that are redeemable only at specific locations and for specific services. An indemnity plan covers your pet at almost all veterinary, specialty and emergency practices and is an

excellent way to manage your pet's ongoing healthcare needs.

VACCINATIONS AND INFECTIOUS DISEASES

There has never been an easier time to prevent a variety of infectious diseases in your dog, but the advances we've made in veterinary medicine come with a price—choice. Now while it may seem that this is a good thing, it also has never been more difficult for the pet owner (or the vet) to make an informed decision about the best way to protect pets through vaccination.

Years ago, it was just accepted that puppies got a starter series of vaccinations and then annual "boosters" throughout their lives to keep them protected. As more and more vaccines became available, consumers wanted the convenience of having all of that protection in a single injection. The result was "multivalent" vaccines that crammed a lot of protection into a single syringe. The manufacturers' recommendations were to give the vaccines annually, and this was a simple enough protocol to follow. However, as veterinary medicine has become more sophisticated and we have started looking more at healthcare quandaries rather than convenience, it became necessary to reevaluate the situation and deal with some tough questions. It is important to realize that whether

COMMON INFECTIOUS DISEASES

Let's discuss some of the diseases that create the need for vaccination in the first place. Following are the major canine infectious diseases and a simple explanation of each.

Rabies: A devastating viral disease that can be fatal in dogs and people. In fact, vaccination of dogs and cats is an important public-health measure to create a resistant animal buffer population to protect people from contracting the disease. Vaccination schedules are determined on a government level and are not optional for pet owners; rabies vaccination is required by law in all 50 states.

Parvovirus: A severe, potentially life-threatening disease that is easily transmitted between dogs. There are four strains of the virus, but it is believed that there is significant "cross-protection" between strains that may be included in individual vaccines.

Distemper: A potentially severe and life-threatening disease with a relatively high risk of exposure, especially in certain regions. In very high-risk distemper environments, young pups may be vaccinated with human measles vaccine, a related virus that offers cross-protection when administered at four to ten weeks of age.

Hepatitis: Caused by canine type 1 (CAV-1), but since vaccination with the causative virus has a higher rate of adverse effects, cross-protection is derived from the use of adenovirus type 2 (CAV-2), a cause of respiratory disease and one of the potential causes of canine cough. Vaccination with CAV-2 provides long-term immunity against hepatitis, but relatively less protection against respiratory infection.

Canine cough: Also called tracheobronchitis, actually a fairly complicated result of viral and bacterial offenders; therefore, even with vaccination, protection is incomplete. Wherever dogs congregate, canine cough will likely be spread among them. Intranasal vaccination with *Bordetella* and parainfluenza is the best safeguard, but the duration of immunity does not appear to be very long, typically a year at most. These are non-core vaccines, but vaccination is sometimes mandated by boarding kennels, obedience classes, dog shows and other places where dogs congregate to try to minimize spread of infection.

Leptospirosis: A potentially fatal disease that is more common in some geographic regions. It is capable of being spread to humans. The disease varies with the individual "serovar," or strain, of *Leptospira* involved. Since there does not appear to be much cross-protection between serovars, protection is only as good as the likelihood that the serovar in the vaccine is the same as the one in the pet's local environment. Problems with *Leptospira* vaccines are that protection does not last very long, side effects are not uncommon and a large percentage of dogs (perhaps 30%) may not respond to vaccination.

Borrelia burgdorferi: The cause of Lyme disease, the risk of which varies with the geographic area in which the pet lives and travels. Lyme disease is spread by deer ticks in the eastern US and western black-legged ticks in the western part of the country, and the risk of exposure is high in some regions. Lameness, fever and inappetence are most commonly seen in affected dogs. The extent of protection from the vaccine has not been conclusively demonstrated.

Coronavirus: This disease has a high risk of exposure, especially in areas where dogs congregate, but it typically causes only mild to moderate digestive upset (diarrhea, vomiting, etc.). Vaccines are available, but the duration of protection is believed to be relatively short and the effectiveness of the vaccine in preventing infection is considered low.

There are many other vaccinations available, including those for *Giardia* and canine adenovirus-1. While there may be some specific indications for their use, and local risk factors to be considered, they are not widely recommended for most dogs.

or not to use a particular vaccine depends on the risk of contracting the disease against which it protects, the severity of the disease if it is contracted, the duration of immunity provided by the vaccine, the safety of the product and the needs of the individual animal. In a

very general sense, rabies, distemper, hepatitis and parvovirus are considered core vaccine needs, while parainfluenza, *Bordetella bronchiseptica*, leptospirosis, coronavirus and borreliosis (Lyme disease) are considered non-core needs and best reserved for animals that demonstrate reasonable risk of contracting the diseases.

PROBLEM: AND THAT STARTS WITH "P"

Urinary tract problems more commonly affect female dogs, especially those who have been spayed. The first sign that a urinary tract problem exists usually is a strong odor from the urine or an unusual color. Blood in the urine, known as hematuria, is another sign of an infection, related to cystitis, a bladder infection, bladder cancer or a blood-clotting disorder. Urinary tract problems can also be signaled by the dog's straining while urinating, experiencing pain during urination and genital discharge as well as excessive water intake and urination.

Excessive drinking, in and of itself, does not indicate a urinary tract problem. A dog who is drinking more than normal may have a kidney or liver problem, a hormonal disorder or diabetes mellitus. Behaviorists report a disorder known as psychogenic polydipsia, which manifests itself in excessive drinking and urination. If you notice your dog drinking much more than normal, take him to the vet.

NEUTERING/SPAYING

Sterilization procedures (neutering for males/spaying for females) are meant to accomplish several purposes. While the underlying premise is to address the risk of pet overpopulation, there are also some medical and behavioral benefits to the surgeries. For females, spaying prior to the first estrus (heat cycle) leads to a marked reduction in the risk of mammary cancer and other serious female problems. There also will be no manifestations of "heat" to attract male dogs and no bleeding in the house. For males, there is prevention of testicular cancer and a reduction in the risk of prostate problems. In both sexes there may be some limited reduction in aggressive behaviors toward other dogs, and some diminishing of urine marking, roaming and mounting.

While neutering and spaying do indeed prevent animals from contributing to pet overpopulation, even no-cost and low-cost neutering options have not eliminated the problem. Perhaps one of the main reasons for this is that individuals that intentionally breed their dogs and those that allow their animals to run at large are the main causes of unwanted offspring. Also, animals in shelters are often there because they were abandoned or relinquished, not because they came from unplanned matings. Neutering/spaying is important, but it should be considered in the context of the real causes of animals' ending up in shelters and eventually being euthanized.

One of the important considerations regarding neutering is that it is a surgical procedure. This sometimes gets lost in discussions of low-cost procedures and commoditization of the process. In females, spaying is specifically referred to as an ovariohysterectomy. In this procedure, a midline incision is made in the abdomen and the entire uterus and both ovaries are surgically removed. While this is a major invasive surgical procedure, it usually has few complications because it is typically performed on healthy young animals. However, it is major surgery, as any woman who has had a hysterectomy will attest.

In males, neutering has traditionally referred to castration, which involves the surgical removal of both testicles. While still a significant piece of surgery, there is not the abdominal exposure that is required in the female surgery. In addition, there is now a chemical

Taking time to smell the flowers can make a dog sneeze! Just like people, dogs can have reactions to pollen, grasses and other allergens outdoors.

sterilization option, in which a solution is injected into each testicle, leading to atrophy of the sperm-producing cells. This can typically be done under sedation rather than full anesthesia. This is a relatively new approach, and there are no long-term clinical studies yet available.

Neutering/spaying is typically done around six months of age at most veterinary hospitals, although techniques have been pioneered to perform the procedures in animals as young as eight weeks of age. In general, the surgeries on the very young animals are done for the specific reason of sterilizing them before they go to their new homes. This is done in some shelter hospitals for assurance that the animals will definitely not produce any pups. Otherwise, these organizations need to rely on owners to comply with their wishes to have the animals "altered" at a later date, something that does not always happen.

S.E.M. BY DR. DENNIS KUNKEL, UNIVERSITY OF HAWAII

*A scanning electron micrograph of a dog flea, **Ctenocephalides canis**, on dog hair.*

EXTERNAL PARASITES

FLEAS

Fleas have been around for millions of years and, while we have better tools now for controlling them than at any time in the past, there still is little chance that they will end up on an endangered species list. Actually, they are very well adapted to living on our pets, and they continue to adapt as we make advances.

The female flea can consume 15 times her weight in blood during active reproduction and can lay as many as 40 eggs a day. These eggs are very resistant to the effects of insecticides. They hatch into larvae, which then mature and spin cocoons. The immature fleas reside in this pupal stage until the time is right for feeding. This pupal stage is also very resistant to the effects of insecticides, and pupae can last in the environment without feeding for many months. Newly emergent fleas are attracted to animals by the warmth of the animals' bodies, movement and exhaled carbon dioxide. However, when they first emerge from their cocoons, they orient towards light; thus when an animal passes between a flea and the light source, casting a shadow, the flea pounces and starts to feed. If the animal turns out to be a dog or cat, the reproductive cycle continues. If the flea lands on another type of animal, including a person, the flea will bite but will then look for a more appropriate host. An emerging adult flea can survive without feeding for up to 12 months but, once it tastes blood, it can survive off its host for only 3 to 4 days.

It was once thought that fleas spend most of their lives in the environment, but we now know that fleas won't willingly jump off a dog unless leaping to another dog or when physically removed by brushing, bathing or other manipulation. Flea eggs, on the other hand, are shiny and smooth, and they roll off the animal and into the environment. The eggs, larvae and pupae then exist in the environment, but once the adult finds a susceptible animal, it's home sweet home until the flea is forced to seek refuge elsewhere.

Since adult fleas live on the animal and immature forms survive in the environment, a successful treatment plan must address all stages of the flea life cycle. There are now several safe and effective flea-control products that can be applied on a monthly

FLEA PREVENTION FOR YOUR DOG

- Discuss with your veterinarian the safest product to protect your dog, likely in the form of a monthly tablet or a liquid preparation placed on the back of the dog's neck.
- For dogs suffering from flea-bite dermatitis, a shampoo or topical insecticide treatment is required.
- Your lawn and property should be sprayed with an insecticide designed to kill fleas and ticks that lurk outdoors.
- Using a flea comb, check the dog's coat regularly for any signs of parasites.
- Practice good housekeeping. Vacuum floors, carpets and furniture regularly, especially in the areas that the dog frequents, and wash the dog's bedding weekly.
- Follow up house-cleaning with carpet shampoos and sprays to rid the house of fleas at all stages of development. Insect growth regulators are the safest option.

basis. These include fipronil, imidacloprid, selamectin and permethrin (found in several formulations). Most of these products have significant flea-killing rates within 24 hours. However, none of them will control the immature forms in the environment. To accomplish this, there are a variety of insect growth regulators that can be

THE FLEA'S LIFE CYCLE

What came first, the flea or the egg? This age-old mystery is more difficult to comprehend than the actual cycle of the flea. Fleas usually live only about four months. A female can lay 2,000 eggs in her lifetime.

Egg

PHOTO BY CAROLINA BIOLOGICAL SUPPLY CO.

After ten days of rolling around your carpet or under your furniture, the eggs hatch into larvae, which feed on various and sundry debris. In days or months, depending on the climate, the larvae spin cocoons and develop into the pupal or nymph stage, which quickly develop into fleas.

Larva

PHOTO BY CAROLINA BIOLOGICAL SUPPLY CO.

Pupa

These immature fleas must locate a host within 10 to 14 days or they will die. Only about 1% of the flea population exist as adult fleas, while the other 99% exist as eggs, larvae or pupae.

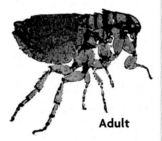

Adult

KILL FLEAS THE NATURAL WAY

If you choose not to go the route of conventional medication, there are some natural ways to ward off fleas:

- Dust your dog with a natural flea powder, composed of such herbal goodies as rosemary, wormwood, pennyroyal, citronella, rue, tobacco powder and eucalyptus.
- Apply diatomaceous earth, the fossilized remains of single-cell algae, to your carpets, furniture and pet's bedding. Even though it's not good for dogs, it's even worse for fleas, which will dry up swiftly and die.
- Brush your dog frequently, give him adequate exercise and let him fast occasionally. All of these activities strengthen the dog's immune system and make him more resistant to disease and parasites.
- Bathe your dog with a capful of pennyroyal or eucalyptus oil.
- Feed a natural diet, free of additives and preservatives. Add some fresh garlic and brewer's yeast to the dog's morning portion, as these items have flea-repelling properties.

sprayed into the environment (e.g., pyriproxyfen, methoprene, fenoxycarb) as well as insect development inhibitors such as lufenuron that can be administered. These compounds have no effect on adult fleas, but they stop immature forms from developing into adults. In years gone by, we relied heavily on toxic insecticides (such as organophosphates, organochlorines and carbamates) to manage the flea problem, but today's options are not only much safer to use on our pets but also safer for the environment.

TICKS

Ticks are members of the spider class (arachnids) and are blood-sucking parasites capable of transmitting a variety of diseases, including Lyme disease, ehrlichiosis, babesiosis and Rocky Mountain spotted fever. It's easy to see ticks on your own skin, but it is more of a challenge when your furry companion is affected. Whenever you happen to be planning a stroll in a tick-infested area (especially forests, grassy or wooded areas or parks) be prepared to do a thorough inspection of your dog afterward to search for ticks. Ticks can be tricky, so make sure you spend time looking in the ears, between the toes and everywhere else where a tick might hide. Ticks need to be attached for 24–72 hours before they transmit most of the diseases that they carry, so you do have a window of opportunity for some preventive intervention.

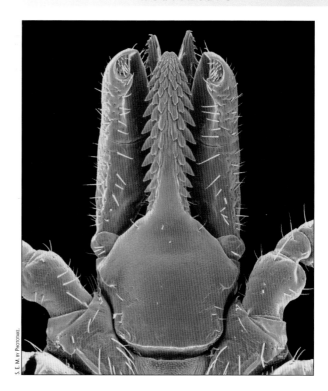

S. E. M. BY PHOTOTAKE.

A scanning electron micrograph of the head of a female deer tick, *Ixodes dammini*, a parasitic tick that carries Lyme disease.

A TICKING BOMB

There is nothing good about a tick's harpooning his nose into your dog's skin. Among the diseases caused by ticks are Rocky Mountain spotted fever, canine ehrlichiosis, canine babesiosis, canine hepatozoonosis and Lyme disease. If a dog is allergic to the saliva of a female wood tick, he can develop tick paralysis.

Female ticks live to eat and breed. They can lay between 4,000 and 5,000 eggs and they die soon after. Males, on the other hand, live only to mate with the females and continue the process as long as they are able. Most ticks live on multiple hosts before parasitizing dogs. The immature forms typically reside on grass and shrubs, waiting for susceptible animals to walk by. The larvae and nymph stages typically feed on wildlife.

If only a few ticks are present on a dog, they can be plucked out, but it is important to remove the entire head and mouthparts,

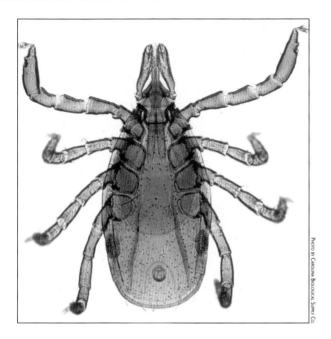

Photo by Carolina Biological Supply Co.

Deer tick,
Ixodes dammini.

disposed of in a container of alcohol or household bleach.

Some of the newer flea products, specifically those with fipronil, selamectin and permethrin, have effect against some, but not all, species of tick. Flea collars containing appropriate pesticides (e.g., propoxur, chlorfenvinphos) can aid in tick control. In most areas, such collars should be placed on animals in March, at the beginning of the tick season, and changed regularly. Leaving the collar on when the pesticide level is waning invites the development of resistance. Amitraz collars are also good for tick control, and the active ingredient does not interfere with other flea-control products. The ingredient helps prevent the attachment of ticks to the skin and will cause those ticks already on the skin to detach themselves.

which may be deeply embedded in the skin. This is best accomplished with forceps designed especially for this purpose; fingers can be used but should be protected with rubber gloves, plastic wrap or at least a paper towel. The tick should be grasped as closely as possible to the animal's skin and should be pulled upward with steady, even pressure. Do not squeeze, crush or puncture the body of the tick or you risk exposure to any disease carried by that tick. Once the ticks have been removed, the sites of attachment should be disinfected. Your hands should then be washed with soap and water to further minimize risk of contagion. The tick should be

TICK CONTROL

Removal of underbrush and leaf litter and the thinning of trees in areas where tick control is desired are recommended. These actions remove the cover and food sources for small animals that serve as hosts for ticks. With continued mowing of grasses in these areas, the probability of ticks' surviving is further reduced. A variety of insecticide ingredients (e.g., resmethrin, carbaryl, permethrin, chlorpyrifos, dioxathion and allethrin) are registered for tick control around the home.

MITES

Mites are tiny arachnid parasites that parasitize the skin of dogs. Skin diseases caused by mites are referred to as "mange," and there are many different forms seen in dogs. These forms are very different from one another, each one warranting an individual description.

Sarcoptic mange, or scabies, is one of the itchiest conditions that affects dogs. The microscopic *Sarcoptes* mites burrow into the superficial layers of the skin and can drive dogs crazy with itchiness. They are also communicable to people, although they can't complete their reproductive cycle on people. In addition to being tiny, the mites also are often difficult to find when trying to make a diagnosis. Skin scrapings from multiple areas are examined microscopically but, even then, sometimes the mites cannot be found.

Fortunately, scabies is relatively easy to treat, and there are a variety of products that will successfully kill the mites. Since the mites can't live in the environment for very long without feeding, a complete cure is usually possible within four to eight weeks.

Cheyletiellosis is caused by a relatively large mite, which sometimes can be seen even without a microscope. Often referred to as "walking dandruff," this also causes itching, but not usually as profound as with scabies.

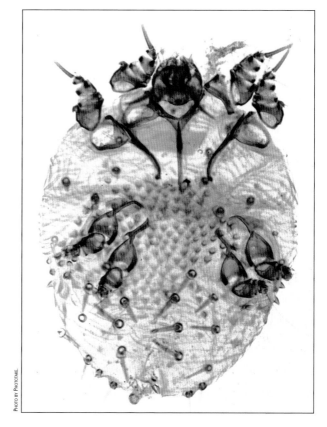

PHOTO BY PHOTOTAKE.

Sarcoptes scabiei, commonly known as the "itch mite."

While *Cheyletiella* mites can survive somewhat longer in the environment than scabies mites, they too are relatively easy to treat, being responsive to not only the medications used to treat scabies but also often to flea-control products.

Otodectes cynotis is the canine ear mite and is one of the more common causes of mange, especially in young dogs in shelters or pet stores. That's because the mites are typically present in large numbers and are quickly spread to

Micrograph of a dog louse, *Heterodoxus spiniger.* Female lice attach their eggs to the hairs of the dog. As the eggs hatch, the larval lice bite and feed on the blood. Lice can also feed on dead skin and hair. This feeding activity can cause hair loss and skin problems.

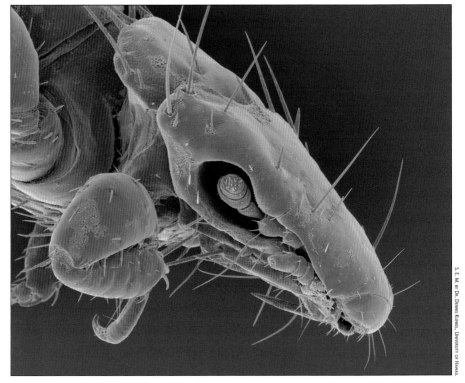

nearby animals. The mites rarely do much harm but can be difficult to eradicate if the treatment regimen is not comprehensive. While many try to treat the condition with ear drops only, this is the most common cause of treatment failure. Ear drops cause the mites to simply move out of the ears and as far away as possible (usually to the base of the tail) until the insecticide levels in the ears drop to an acceptable level—then it's back to business as usual! The successful treatment of ear mites requires treating all animals in the household with a systemic insecticide, such as selamectin, or a combination of miticidal ear drops combined with whole-body flea-control preparations.

Demodicosis, sometimes referred to as red mange, can be one of the most difficult forms of mange to treat. Part of the problem has to do with the fact that the mites live in the hair follicles and they are relatively well shielded from topical and systemic products. The main issue, however, is that demodectic mange typically results only when there is some underlying process interfering with the dog's immune system.

Since *Demodex* mites are

normal residents of the skin of mammals, including humans, there is usually a mite population explosion only when the immune system fails to keep the number of mites in check. In young animals, the immune deficit may be transient or may reflect an actual inherited immune problem. In older animals, demodicosis is usually seen only when there is another disease hampering the immune system, such as diabetes, cancer, thyroid problems or the use of immune-suppressing drugs. Accordingly, treatment involves not only trying to kill the mange mites but also discerning what is interfering with immune function and correcting it if possible.

Chiggers represent several different species of mite that don't parasitize dogs specifically, but do latch on to passersby and can cause irritation. The problem is most prevalent in wooded areas in the late summer and fall. Treatment is not difficult, as the mites do not complete their life cycle on dogs and are susceptible to a variety of miticidal products.

MOSQUITOES

Mosquitoes have long been known to transmit a variety of diseases to people, as well as just being biting pests during warm weather. They also pose a real risk to pets. Not only

do they carry deadly heartworms but recently there also has been much concern over their involvement with West Nile virus. While we can avoid heartworm with the use of preventive medications, there are no such preventives for West Nile virus. The only method of prevention in endemic areas is active mosquito control. Fortunately, most dogs that have been exposed to the virus only developed flu-like symptoms and, to date, there have not been the large number of reported deaths in canines as seen in some other species.

Illustration of *Demodex folliculoram.*

ILLUSTRATION BY PHOTOTAKE

MOSQUITO REPELLENT

Low concentrations of DEET (less than 10%), found in many human mosquito repellents, have been safely used in dogs but, in these concentrations, probably give only about two hours of protection. DEET may be safe in these small concentrations, but since it is not licensed for use on dogs, there is no research proving its safety for dogs. Products containing permethrin give the longest-lasting protection, perhaps two to four weeks. As DEET is not licensed for use on dogs, and both DEET and permethrin can be quite toxic to cats, appropriate care should be exercised. Other products, such as those containing oil of citronella, also have some mosquito-repellent activity, but typically have a relatively short duration of action.

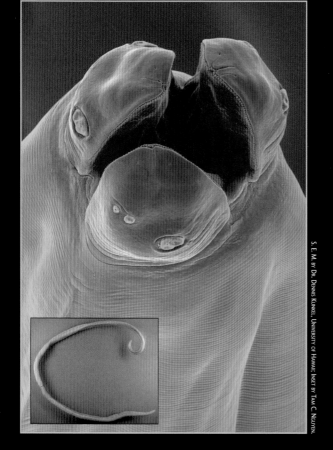

The ascarid roundworm *Toxocara canis,* showing the mouth with three lips. INSET: Photomicrograph of the roundworm *Ascaris lumbricoides.*

S. E. M. BY DR. DENNIS KUNKEL, UNIVERSITY OF HAWAII; INSET BY TAM C. NGUYEN

INTERNAL PARASITES: WORMS

ASCARIDS

Ascarids are intestinal roundworms that rarely cause severe disease in dogs. Nonetheless, they are of major public health significance because they can be transferred to people. Sadly, it is children who are most commonly affected by the parasite, probably from inadvertently ingesting ascarid-contaminated soil. In fact, many yards and children's sandboxes contain appreciable numbers of ascarid eggs. So, while ascarids don't bite dogs or latch onto their intestines to suck blood, they do cause some nasty medical conditions in children and are best eradicated from our furry friends. Because pups can start passing ascarid eggs by three weeks of age, most parasite-control programs begin at two weeks of age and are repeated every two weeks until pups are eight weeks old. It is important to

HOOKED ON ANCYLOSTOMA

Adult dogs can become infected by the bloodsucking nematodes we commonly call hookworms via ingesting larvae from the ground or via the larvae penetrating the dog's skin. It is not uncommon for infected dogs to show no symptoms of hookworm infestation. Sometimes symptoms occur within ten days of exposure. These symptoms can include bloody diarrhea, anemia, loss of weight and general weakness. Dogs pass the hookworm eggs in their stools, which serves as the vet's method of identifying the infestation. The hookworm larvae can encyst themselves in the dog's tissues and be released when the dog is experiencing stress.

Caused by an *Ancylostoma* species whose common host is the dog, cutaneous larval migrans affects humans, causing itching and lumps and streaks beneath the surface of the skin.

S. E. M. BY DR. DENNIS KUNKEL, UNIVERSITY OF HAWAII.

realize that bitches can pass ascarids to their pups even if they test negative prior to whelping. Accordingly, bitches are best treated at the same time as the pups.

HOOKWORMS

Unlike ascarids, hookworms do latch onto a dog's intestinal tract and can cause significant loss of blood and protein. Similar to ascarids, hookworms can be transmitted to humans, where they cause a condition known as cutaneous larval migrans. Dogs can become infected either by consuming the infective larvae or by the larvae's penetrating the skin directly. People most often get infected when they are lying on the ground (such as on a beach) and the larvae penetrate the skin. Yes, the larvae can penetrate through a beach blanket. Hookworms are typically suscep-tible to the same medications used to treat ascarids.

The hookworm *Ancylostoma caninum* infests the intestines of dogs. INSET: Note the row of hooks at the posterior end, used to anchor the worm to the intestinal wall.

WHIPWORMS

Whipworms latch onto the lower aspects of the dog's colon and can cause cramping and diarrhea. Eggs do not start to appear in the dog's feces until about three months after the dog was infected. This worm has a peculiar life cycle, which makes it more difficult to control than ascarids or hookworms. The good thing is that whipworms rarely are transferred to people.

Some of the medications used to treat ascarids and hookworms are also effective against whipworms, but, in general, a separate treatment protocol is needed. Since most of the medications are effective against the adults but not the eggs or larvae, treatment is typically repeated in three weeks, and then often in three

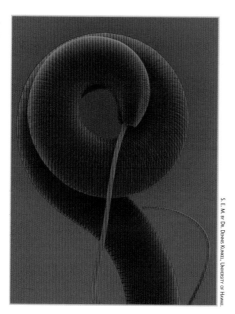

Adult whipworm, *Trichuris* sp., an intestinal parasite.

S.E.M. BY DR. DENNIS KUNKEL, UNIVERSITY OF HAWAII.

> ## WORM-CONTROL GUIDELINES
> - Practice sanitary habits with your dog and home.
> - Clean up after your dog and don't let him sniff or eat other dogs' droppings.
> - Control insects and fleas in the dog's environment. Fleas, lice, cockroaches, beetles, mice and rats can act as hosts for various worms.
> - Prevent dogs from eating uncooked meat, raw poultry and dead animals.
> - Keep dogs and children from playing in sand and soil.
> - Kennel dogs on cement or gravel; avoid dirt runs.
> - Administer heartworm preventives regularly.
> - Have your vet examine your dog's stools at your annual visits.
> - Select a boarding kennel carefully so as to avoid contamination from other dogs or an unsanitary environment.
> - Prevent dogs from roaming. Obey local leash laws.

months as well. Unfortunately, since dogs don't develop resistance to whipworms, it is difficult to prevent them from getting reinfected if they visit soil contaminated with whipworm eggs.

TAPEWORMS

There are many different species of tapeworm that affect dogs, but *Dipylidium caninum* is probably the most common and is spread by fleas. Flea larvae feed on organic debris and tapeworm eggs in the environment and, when a dog chews at himself and manages to ingest fleas, he might get a dose of tapeworm at the same time. The tapeworm then develops further in the intestine of the dog.

The tapeworm itself, which is a parasitic flatworm that latches onto the intestinal wall, is composed of numerous segments. When the segments break off into the intestine (as proglottids), they may accumulate around the rectum, like grains of rice. While this tapeworm is disgusting in its behavior, it is not directly communicable to humans (although humans can also get infected by swallowing fleas).

A much more dangerous tapeworm is *Echinococcus multilocularis*, which is typically found in foxes, coyotes and wolves. The eggs are passed in the feces and infect rodents, and, when dogs eat the rodents, the dogs can be infected by thousands of adult tapeworms. While the parasites don't cause many problems in dogs, this is considered the most lethal worm infection that people can get. Take appropriate precautions if you live in an area in which these tapeworms are found. Do not use mulch that may contain feces of dogs, cats or wildlife, and

discourage your pets from hunting wildlife. Treat these tapeworm infections aggressively in pets, because if humans get infected, approximately half die.

HEARTWORMS

Heartworm disease is caused by the parasite *Dirofilaria immitis* and is seen in dogs around the world. A member of the roundworm group, it is spread between dogs by the bite of an infected mosquito. The mosquito injects infective larvae into the dog's skin with its bite, and these larvae develop under the skin for a period of time before making their way to the heart. There they develop into adults, which grow and create blockages of the heart, lungs and major blood vessels there. They also start producing offspring (microfilariae),

A dog tapeworm proglottid (body segment).

The dog tapeworm *Taenia pisiformis.*

S. E. M. BY DR. DENNIS KUNKEL, UNIVERSITY OF HAWAII.

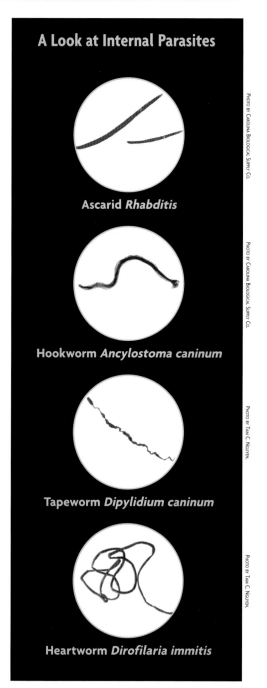

A Look at Internal Parasites

Ascarid *Rhabditis*

Hookworm *Ancylostoma caninum*

Tapeworm *Dipylidium caninum*

Heartworm *Dirofilaria immitis*

Photo by Carolina Biological Supply Co.

Photo by Carolina Biological Supply Co.

Photo by Tam C. Nguyen.

Photo by Tam C. Nguyen.

and these microfilariae circulate in the bloodstream, waiting to hitch a ride when the next mosquito bites. Once in the mosquito, the microfilariae develop into infective larvae and the entire process is repeated.

When dogs get infected with heartworm, over time they tend to develop symptoms associated with heart disease, such as coughing, exercise intolerance and potentially many other manifestations. Diagnosis is confirmed by either seeing the microfilariae themselves in blood samples or using immunologic tests (antigen testing) to identify the presence of adult heartworms. Since antigen tests measure the presence of adult heartworms and microfilarial tests measure offspring produced by adults, neither are positive until six to seven months after the initial infection. However, the beginning of damage can occur by fifth-stage larvae as early as three months after infection. Thus it is possible for dogs to be harboring problem-causing larvae for up to three months before either type of test would identify an infection.

The good news is that there are great protocols available for preventing heartworm in dogs. Testing is critical in the process, and it is important to understand the benefits as well as the limitations of such testing. All dogs six months of age or older that have not been on continuous heartworm-preventive medication should be

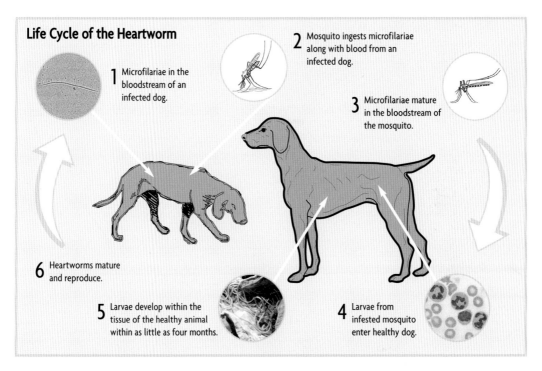

Life Cycle of the Heartworm

1 Microfilariae in the bloodstream of an infected dog.

2 Mosquito ingests microfilariae along with blood from an infected dog.

3 Microfilariae mature in the bloodstream of the mosquito.

4 Larvae from infested mosquito enter healthy dog.

5 Larvae develop within the tissue of the healthy animal within as little as four months.

6 Heartworms mature and reproduce.

screened with microfilarial or antigen tests. For dogs receiving preventive medication, periodic antigen testing helps assess the effectiveness of the preventives. The American Heartworm Society guidelines suggest that annual retesting may not be necessary when owners have absolutely provided continuous heartworm prevention. Retesting on a two- to three-year interval may be sufficient in these cases. However, your veterinarian will likely have specific guidelines under which heartworm preventives will be prescribed, and many prefer to err on the side of safety and retest annually.

It is indeed fortunate that heartworm is relatively easy to prevent, because treatments can be as life-threatening as the disease itself. Treatment requires a two-step process that kills the adult heartworms first and then the microfilariae. Prevention is obviously preferable; this involves a once-monthly oral or topical treatment. The most common oral preventives include ivermectin (not suitable for some breeds), moxidectin and milbemycin oxime; the once-a-month topical drug selamectin provides heartworm protection in addition to flea, some types of tick and other parasite controls.

THE **ABC**S OF
Emergency Care

Abrasions
Clean wound with running water or 3% hydrogen peroxide. Pat dry with gauze and spray with antibiotic. Do not cover.

Animal Bites
Clean area with soap and saline solution or water. Apply pressure to any bleeding area. Apply antibiotic ointment. Identify animal and contact the vet.

Antifreeze Poisoning
Induce vomiting and take dog to the vet.

Bee Sting
Remove stinger and apply soothing lotion or cold compress; give antihistamine in proper dosage.

Bleeding
Apply pressure directly to wound with gauze or towel for five to ten minutes. If wound does not stop bleeding, wrap wound with gauze and adhesive tape.

Bloat/Gastric Torsion
Immediately take the dog to the vet or emergency clinic; phone from car. No time to waste.

Burns
Chemical: Bathe dog with water and pet shampoo. Rinse in saline solution. Apply antibiotic ointment.

Acid: Rinse with water. Apply one part baking soda, two parts water to affected area.

Alkali: Rinse with water. Apply one part vinegar, four parts water to affected area.

Electrical: Apply antibiotic ointment. Seek veterinary assistance immediately.

Choking
If the dog is on the verge of collapsing, wedge a solid object, such as the handle of a screwdriver, between molars on one side of the mouth to keep mouth open. Pull tongue out. Use long-nosed pliers or fingers to remove foreign object. Do not push the object down the dog's throat. For small or medium dogs, hold dog upside down by hind legs and shake firmly to dislodge foreign object.

Chlorine Ingestion
With clean water, rinse the mouth and eyes. Give the dog water to drink; contact the vet.

Constipation
Feed dog 2 tablespoons bran flakes with each meal. Encourage drinking water. Mix $1/4$-teaspoon mineral oil in dog's food. Contact vet if persists longer than 24 hours.

Diarrhea
Withhold food for 12 to 24 hours. Feed dog anti-diarrheal with eyedropper. When feeding resumes, feed one part boiled hamburger, one part plain cooked rice, $1/4$- to $3/4$-cup four times daily. Contact vet if persists longer than 24 hours.

Dog Bite
Snip away hair around puncture wound; clean with 3% hydrogen peroxide; apply tincture of iodine. Identify biting dog and contact the vet. If wound appears deep, take the dog to the vet.

Frostbite
Wrap the dog in a heavy blanket. Warm affected area with a warm bath for ten minutes. Red color to skin will return with circulation; if tissues are pale after 20 minutes, contact the vet.

Use a portable, durable container large enough to contain all items.

Heat Stroke
Partially submerge the dog in cold water; if no response within ten minutes, contact the vet.

Hot Spots
Mix 2 packets Domeboro® with 2 cups water. Saturate cloth with mixture and apply to hot spots for 15 to 30 minutes. Apply antibiotic ointment. Repeat every six to eight hours.

Poisonous Plants
Wash affected area with soap and water. Cleanse with alcohol. For foxtail/grass, apply antibiotic ointment. Contact the vet if plant is ingested.

Rat Poison Ingestion
Induce vomiting. Keep dog calm, maintain dog's normal body temperature (use blanket or heating pad). Get to the vet for antidote.

Shock
Keep the dog calm and warm; call for veterinary assistance.

Snake Bite
If possible, bandage the area and apply pressure. If the area is not conducive to bandaging, use ice to control bleeding. Get immediate help from the vet.

Tick Removal
Apply flea and tick spray directly on tick. Wait one minute. Using tweezers or wearing plastic gloves, apply constant pull while grasping tick's body. Apply antibiotic ointment.

Vomiting
Restrict dog's water intake; offer a few ice cubes. Withhold food for next meal. Contact vet if vomiting persists longer than 24 hours.

DOG OWNER'S FIRST-AID KIT

- ❑ **Gauze bandages/swabs**
- ❑ **Adhesive and non-adhesive bandages**
- ❑ **Antibiotic powder**
- ❑ **Antiseptic wash**
- ❑ **Hydrogen peroxide 3%**
- ❑ **Antibiotic ointment**
- ❑ **Lubricating jelly**
- ❑ **Rectal thermometer**
- ❑ **Nylon muzzle**
- ❑ **Scissors and forceps**
- ❑ **Eyedropper**
- ❑ **Syringe**
- ❑ **Anti-bacterial/fungal solution**
- ❑ **Saline solution**
- ❑ **Antihistamine**
- ❑ **Cotton balls**
- ❑ **Nail clippers**
- ❑ **Screwdriver/pen knife**
- ❑ **Flashlight**
- ❑ **Emergency phone numbers**

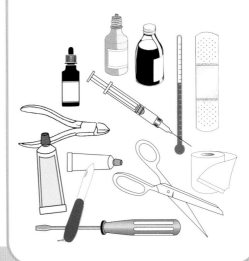

Number-One Killer Disease in Dogs: CANCER

In every age, there is a word associated with a disease or plague that causes humans to shudder. In the 21st century, that word is "cancer." Just as cancer is the leading cause of death in humans, it claims nearly half the lives of dogs that die from a natural disease as well as half the dogs that die over the age of ten years.

Described as a genetic disease, cancer becomes a greater risk as the dog ages. Vets and dog owners have become increasingly aware of the threat of cancer to dogs. Statistics reveal that one dog in every five will develop cancer, the most common of which is skin cancer. Many cancers, including prostate, ovarian and breast cancer, can be avoided by spaying and neutering our dogs by the age of six months.

Early detection of cancer can save or extend a dog's life, so it is absolutely vital for owners to have their dogs examined by a qualified vet or oncologist immediately upon detection of any abnormality. Certain dietary guidelines have also proven to reduce the onset and spread of cancer. Foods based on fish rather than beef, due to the presence of Omega-3 fatty acids, are recommended. Other amino acids such as glutamine have significant benefits for canines, particularly those breeds that show a greater susceptibility to cancer.

Cancer management and treatments promise hope for future generations of canines. Since the disease is genetic, breeders should never breed a dog whose parents, grandparents and any related siblings have developed cancer. It is difficult to know whether to exclude an otherwise healthy dog from a breeding program, as the disease does not manifest itself until the dog's senior years.

RECOGNIZE CANCER WARNING SIGNS

Since early detection can possibly rescue your dog from becoming a cancer statistic, it is essential for owners to recognize the possible signs and seek the assistance of a qualified professional.

- Abnormal bumps or lumps that continue to grow
- Bleeding or discharge from any body cavity
- Persistent stiffness or lameness
- Recurrent sores or sores that do not heal
- Inappetence
- Breathing difficulties
- Weight loss
- Bad breath or odors
- General malaise and fatigue
- Eating and swallowing problems
- Difficulty urinating and defecating

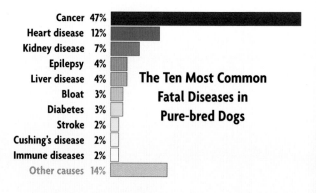

Cancer	47%
Heart disease	12%
Kidney disease	7%
Epilepsy	4%
Liver disease	4%
Bloat	3%
Diabetes	3%
Stroke	2%
Cushing's disease	2%
Immune diseases	2%
Other causes	14%

The Ten Most Common Fatal Diseases in Pure-bred Dogs

Canine Cognitive Dysfunction

"Old-Dog" Syndrome

There are many ways for you to evaluate old-dog syndrome. Veterinarians have defined canine cognitive dysfunction as the gradual deterioration of cognitive abilities, indicated by changes in the dog's behavior. When a dog changes his routine response, and maladies have been eliminated as the cause of these behavioral changes, then canine cognitive dysfunction is the usual diagnosis.

More than half the dogs over eight years old suffer from some form of this syndrome. The older the dog, the more chance he has of suffering from it. In humans, doctors often dismiss the behavioral changes of canine cognitive dysfunction as part of "winding down."

There are four major signs of canine cognitive dysfunction: frequent potty accidents inside the home, sleeping much more or much less than normal, acting confused and failing to respond to social stimuli.

Symptoms

FREQUENT POTTY ACCIDENTS

- Urinates in the house.
- Defecates in the house.
- Doesn't signal that he wants to go out.

FAILURE TO RESPOND TO SOCIAL STIMULI

- Comes to people less frequently, whether called or not.
- Doesn't tolerate petting for more than a short time.
- Doesn't come to the door when you return home.

CONFUSION

- Goes outside and just stands there.
- Appears confused with a faraway look in his eyes.
- Hides more often.
- Doesn't recognize friends.
- Doesn't come when called.
- Walks around listlessly and without a destination.

SLEEP PATTERNS

- Awakens more slowly.
- Sleeps more than normal during the day.
- Sleeps less during the night.

STANDARD SCHNAUZER

When we bring home a puppy, full of the energy and exuberance that accompanies youth, we hope for a long, happy and fulfilling relationship with the new family member. Even when we adopt an older dog, we look forward to the years of companionship ahead with a new canine friend. However, aging is inevitable for all creatures, and there will come a time when your Standard Schnauzer reaches his senior years and will need special considerations and attention to his care.

WHEN IS MY DOG A "SENIOR"?
With excellent-quality dog food readily available, and with regular veterinary care, the average longevity for the breed seems to be around 14 years. It is not unusual for the Standard Schnauzer to live to 16 or 17 years of age. Since the breed is blessed with good health and relative freedom from hereditary problems, most Standard Schnauzers die from "old age" (if that exists!) rather than from health problems. While many breeds are considered seniors at around seven years old, nine or

ten years is more accurate for the Standard Schnauzer.

Obviously, the old "seven dog years to one human year" theory is not exact. In puppyhood, a dog's year is actually comparable to more than seven human years, considering the puppy's rapid growth during his first year. Then, in adulthood, the ratio decreases. Regardless, the more viable rule of thumb is that the larger the dog, the shorter his expected lifespan. Of course, this can vary among individual dogs, with many living longer than expected, which we hope is the case!

WHAT ARE THE SIGNS OF AGING?
By the time your dog has reached his senior years, you will know him very well, so the physical and behavioral changes that accompany aging should be noticeable to you. Humans and dogs share the most obvious physical sign of aging: gray hair! Graying often occurs first on the muzzle and face, around the eyes. Other telltale signs are the dog's overall decrease in activity. Your older dog might be more

content to nap and rest, and he may not show the same old enthusiasm when it's time to play in the yard or go for a walk. Other physical signs include significant weight loss or gain; more labored movement; skin and coat problems, possibly hair loss; sight and/or hearing problems; changes in toileting habits, perhaps seeming "unhousebroken" at times; and tooth decay, bad breath or other mouth problems.

There are behavioral changes that go along with aging, too. There are numerous causes for behavioral changes. Sometimes a dog's apparent confusion results from a physical change like diminished sight or hearing. If his confusion causes him to be

WEATHER WORRIES

Older pets are less tolerant of extremes in weather, both heat and cold. Your older dog should not spend extended periods in the sun; when outdoors in the warm weather, make sure he does not become overheated. In chilly weather, consider a sweater for your dog when outdoors and limit time spent outside. Whether or not his coat is thinning, he will need provisions to keep him warm when the weather is cold. You may even place his bed by a heating duct in your living room or bedroom.

afraid, he may act aggressively or defensively. He may sleep more frequently because his daily walks, though shorter now, tire him out. He may begin to experience separation anxiety or, conversely, become less interested in petting and attention.

There also are clinical conditions that cause behavioral changes in older dogs. One such condition is known as canine cognitive dysfunction (familiarly known as "old-dog" syndrome). It can be frustrating for an owner whose dog is affected with cognitive dysfunction, as it can result in behavioral changes of all types, most seemingly unexplainable. Common changes include the dog's forgetting aspects of the daily routine, such as times to eat, go out for walks, relieve himself and the like. Along the same lines, you may take your dog out at the regular time for a potty trip and he may have no idea why he is there. Sometimes a placid dog will begin to show aggressive or possessive tendencies or, conversely, a hyperactive dog will start to "mellow out."

Disease also can be the cause of behavioral changes in senior dogs. Hormonal problems (Cushing's disease is common in older dogs), diabetes and thyroid disease can cause increased appetite, which can lead to aggression related to food guarding. It's better to be proactive with your senior dog, making more frequent trips to the vet if necessary and having bloodwork done to test for the diseases that can commonly befall older dogs.

This is not to say that, as dogs age, they all fall apart physically and become nasty in personality. The aforementioned changes are discussed to alert owners to the things that may happen as their dogs get older. Many hardy dogs remain active and alert well into old age; Standard Schnauzers are known to remain very active in their senior years. However, it can be frustrating and heartbreaking for owners to see their beloved dogs change physically and temperamentally. Just know that it's the same Standard Schnauzer under there, and that he still loves you and appreciates your care, which he needs now more than ever.

HOW DO I CARE FOR MY AGING DOG?

Again, every dog is an individual in terms of aging. Your dog might reach the estimated "senior" age for his breed and show no signs of slowing down. However, even if he shows no outward signs of aging, he should begin a senior-care program as determined by your vet. He may not show it, but he's not a pup anymore! By

providing him with extra attention to his veterinary care at this age, you will be practicing good preventive medicine, ensuring that the rest of your dog's life will be as long, active, happy and healthy as possible. If you do notice indications of aging, such as graying and/or changes in sleeping, eating or toileting habits, this is a sign to set up a senior-care visit with your vet right away to make sure that these changes are not related to any health problems.

To start, senior dogs should visit the vet twice yearly for exams, routine tests and overall evaluations. Many veterinarians have special screening programs especially for senior dogs that can include a thorough physical exam; blood test to determine complete blood count; serum biochemistry test, which screens for liver, kidney and blood problems as well as cancer; urinalysis; and dental exams. With these tests, it can be determined whether your dog has any health problems; the results also establish a baseline for your pet against which future test results can be compared.

In addition to these tests, your vet may suggest additional testing, including an EKG, tests for glaucoma and other problems of the eye, chest X-rays, screening for tumors, blood pressure test, test for thyroid

AH, MY ACHING BONES!

Senior dogs affected by arthritis may have trouble moving about. If you notice this in your dog, you may have to limit him to one floor of the house so that he does not have to deal with stairs. If there are a few steps leading out into the yard, a ramp may help the dog. Likewise, he may need a ramp or a boost to get in and out of the car. Ensure that he has plenty of soft bedding on which to sleep and rest, as this will be comfortable for his aching joints. Also ensure that surfaces on which the dog walks are not slippery. Investigate new dietary supplements made for arthritic dogs. Talk to your veterinarian about these supplements.

function and screening for parasites and reassessment of his preventive program. Your vet also will ask you questions about your dog's diet and activity level, what you feed and the amounts that you feed. This information, along with his evaluation of the dog's overall condition, will enable him to suggest proper dietary changes, if needed.

This may seem like quite a work-up for your pet, but veterinarians advise that older dogs need more frequent attention so that any health problems can be detected as early as possible. Serious conditions like kidney disease, heart disease and cancer may not present outward symptoms, or the problem may go undetected if the symptoms are mistaken by owners as just part of the aging process.

There are some conditions more common in elderly dogs that are difficult to ignore. Cognitive dysfunction shares much in common with senility and Alzheimer's disease, and dogs are not immune. Dogs can become confused and/or disoriented, lose their house-training, have abnormal sleep-wake cycles and interact differently with their owners. Be heartened by the fact that, in some ways, there are more treatment options for dogs with cognitive dysfunction than for people with similar conditions. There is good evidence that continued stimulation in the form of games, play, training and exercise can help to maintain cognitive function. There are also medications (such as seligiline) and antioxidant-fortified senior diets that have been shown to be beneficial.

Cancer is also a condition more common in the elderly. While lung

Here's hoping that your Standard Schnauzer will be clowning around for many happy, healthy years!

cancer, which is a major killer in humans, is relatively rare in dogs, almost all of the cancers seen in people are also seen in pets. If pets are getting regular physical examinations, cancers are often detected early. There are a variety of cancer therapies available today, and many pets continue to live happy lives with appropriate treatment.

Degenerative joint disease, often referred to as arthritis, is another malady common to both elderly dogs and humans. A lifetime of wear and tear on joints and running around at play eventually takes its toll and results in stiffness and difficulty in getting around. As dogs live longer and healthier lives, it is natural that they should eventually feel some of the effects of aging. Once again, if regular veterinary care has been available, your pet should not have been carrying extra pounds all those years and wearing those joints out before their time. If your pet was unfortunate enough to inherit hip dysplasia, osteochondritis dissecans or any of the other developmental orthopedic diseases, battling the onset of degenerative joint disease was probably a longstanding goal. In any case, there are now many effective remedies for managing degenerative joint disease and a number of remarkable surgeries as well.

Aside from the extra veterinary care, there is much you can do at home to keep your older dog in good condition. The dog's diet is an important factor. If your dog's appetite decreases, he will not be getting the nutrients he needs. He also will lose weight, which is unhealthy for a dog at a proper weight. Conversely, an older dog's metabolism is slower and he usually exercises less, but he should not be allowed to become obese. Obesity in an older dog is

ADAPTING TO AGE

As dogs age and their once-keen senses begin to deteriorate, they can experience stress and confusion. However, dogs are very adaptable, and most can adjust to deficiencies in their sight and hearing. As these processes often deteriorate gradually, the dog makes adjustments gradually, too. Because dogs become so familiar with the layout of their homes and yards, and with their daily routines, they are able to get around even if they cannot see or hear as well. Help your senior dog by keeping things consistent around the house. Keep up with your regular times for walking and potty trips, and do not relocate his crate or rearrange the furniture. Your dog is a very adaptable creature and can make compensation for his diminished ability, but you want to help him along the way and not make changes that will cause him confusion.

especially risky, because extra pounds mean extra stress on the body, increasing his vulnerability to heart disease. Additionally, the extra pounds make it harder for the dog to move about.

You should discuss age-related feeding changes with your vet. For a dog who has lost interest in food, it may be suggested to try some different types of food until you find something new that the dog likes. For an obese dog, a "light"-formula dog food or reducing food portions may be advised, along with exercise appropriate to his physical condition and energy level.

As for exercise, the senior dog should not be allowed to become a "couch potato" despite his old age. He may not be able to handle the morning run, long walks and vigorous games of fetch, but he still needs to get up and get moving. Keep up with your daily walks, but keep the distances shorter and let your dog set the pace. If he gets to the point where he's not up for walks, let him stroll around the yard. On the other hand, as we've mentioned, many Standard Schnauzers remain quite active in their senior years, so base changes to the exercise program on your own individual dog and what he's capable of. Don't worry, your Standard Schnauzer will let you know when it's time to rest.

Keep up with your grooming routine as you always have. Be extra-diligent about checking the skin and coat for problems. Older dogs can experience thinning coats as a normal aging process, but they can also lose hair as a result of medical problems. Some thinning is normal, but patches of baldness or the loss of significant amounts of hair is not.

Hopefully, you've been regular with brushing your dog's teeth throughout his life. Healthy teeth directly affect overall good health. We already know that bacteria from gum infections can enter the dog's body through the damaged gums and travel to the organs. At a stage in life when his organs don't function as well as they used to, you don't want anything to put additional strain on them. Clean teeth also contribute to a healthy immune system. Offering the dental-type chews in addition to toothbrushing can help, as they remove plaque and tartar as the dog chews.

Along with the same good care you've given him all of his life, pay a little extra attention to your dog in his senior years and keep up with twice-yearly trips to the vet. The sooner a problem is uncovered, the greater the chances of a full recovery.

SHOWING YOUR

STANDARD SCHNAUZER

Is dog showing in your blood? Are you excited by the idea of gaiting your handsome Standard Schnauzer around the ring to the thunderous applause of an enthusiastic audience? Are you certain that your beloved Standard Schnauzer is flawless? You are not alone! If this sounds like you, and if you are considering entering your Standard Schnauzer in a dog show, here are some basic questions to ask yourself:

- Did you purchase a "show-quality" puppy from the breeder?
- Is your puppy at least six months of age?
- Does the puppy exhibit correct show type for his breed?
- Does your puppy have any disqualifying faults?
- Is your Standard Schnauzer registered with the American Kennel Club?
- How much time do you have to devote to training, grooming, conditioning and exhibiting your dog?
- Do you understand the rules and regulations of a dog show?
- Do you have time to learn how to show your dog properly?
- Do you have the financial resources to invest in showing your dog?
- Will you show the dog yourself or hire a professional handler?
- Do you have a vehicle that can accommodate your weekend trips to the dog shows?

Success in the show ring requires more than a pretty face, a waggy tail and a pocketful of liver. Even though dog shows can be exciting and enjoyable, the sport of conformation makes great demands on the exhibitors and the dogs. Winning exhibitors live for their dogs, devoting time and money to their dogs' presentation, conditioning and training. Very few novices, even those with good dogs, will find themselves in the winners' circle, though it does happen. Don't be disheartened, though. Every exhibitor began as a novice and worked his way up to the Group ring. It's the "working your way up" part that you must keep in mind.

Assuming that you have purchased a puppy of the correct type and quality for showing, let's begin to examine the world of showing and what's required to get started. Although the entry fee into a dog show is nominal, there are lots of other hidden costs involved with "finishing" your Standard Schnauzer, that is, making him a champion. Things like equipment,

FOR MORE INFORMATION...
For reliable up-to-date information about registration, dog shows and other canine competitions, contact one of the national registries by mail or via the Internet.

American Kennel Club
5580 Centerview Dr., Raleigh, NC 27606-3390
www.akc.org

United Kennel Club
100 E. Kilgore Road, Kalamazoo, MI 49002
www.ukcdogs.com

Canadian Kennel Club
89 Skyway Ave., Suite 100, Etobicoke, Ontario
M9W 6R4 Canada
www.ckc.ca

travel, training and conditioning all cost money. A more serious campaign will include fees for a professional handler, boarding, cross-country travel and advertising. Top-winning show dogs can represent a very considerable invest-ment—over $100,000 has been spent in campaigning some dogs. (The investment can be less, of course, for owners who don't use professional handlers.)

Many owners, on the other hand, enter their "average" Standard Schnauzers in dog shows for the fun and enjoyment of it. Dog showing makes an absorbing hobby, with many rewards for dogs and owners alike. If you're having fun, meeting other people who share your interests and enjoying the overall experience, you likely will catch the "bug." Soon you will be envisioning yourself in the center ring at the Westminster Kennel Club Dog Show in New York City. This magical dog show is televised annually from Madison Square Garden, and the victorious dog becomes a celebrity overnight.

AKC CONFORMATION SHOWING

GETTING STARTED
Visiting a dog show as a spectator is a great place to start. Pick up the show catalog to find out what time your breed is being shown, who is judging the breed and in which ring the classes will be held. To start, Standard Schnauzers compete against other Standard Schnauzers, and the winner is selected as Best of Breed by the judge. This is the procedure for each breed. At a group show, all of the Best of Breed winners go on to compete for Group One (first place) in their respective groups. For example, all Best of Breed winners in a given group compete against each other; this is done for all seven groups. Finally, all seven group winners go head to head in the ring for the Best in Show award.

What most spectators don't understand is the basic idea of conformation. A dog show is often referred as a "conformation" show. This means that the judge should decide how each dog stacks up (conforms) to the breed standard for his given breed: how well does this

Championship runs in the family. Ch. Oakwood April Shower with three of her daughters: Am./Can. Ch. Oakwood Mayflower, Am./Can. Ch. Oakwood Winter Storm and Ch. Oakwood Perfect Season.

Standard Schnauzer conform to the ideal representative detailed in the standard? Ideally, this is what happens. In reality, however, this ideal often gets slighted as the judge compares Standard Schnauzer #1 to Standard Schnauzer #2. Again, the ideal is that each dog is judged based on his merits in comparison to his breed standard, not in comparison to the other dogs in the ring. It is easier for judges to compare dogs of the same breed to decide which they think is the better specimen; in the group and Best in Show rings, however, it is very difficult to compare one breed to another, like apples to oranges. Thus the dog's conformation to the breed standard—not to mention advertising dollars and good handling—is essential to success in conformation shows. The dog described in the standard (the standard for each AKC breed is

written and approved by the breed's national parent club and then submitted to the AKC for approval) is the perfect dog of that breed, and breeders keep their eye on the standard when they choose which dogs to breed, hoping to get closer and closer to the ideal with each litter.

Another good first step for the novice is to join a dog club. You will be astonished by the many and different kinds of dog clubs in the country, with about 5,000 clubs holding events every year. Most clubs require that prospective new members present two letters of recommendation from existing members. Perhaps you've made some friends visiting a show held by a particular club and you would like to join that club. Dog clubs may specialize in a single breed, like a local or regional Standard Schnauzer club, or in a specific pursuit, such as obedience, tracking or herding tests. There are all-breed clubs for all dog enthusiasts; they sponsor special training days, seminars on topics like grooming or handling or lectures on breeding or canine genetics. There are also clubs that specialize in certain types of dogs, like working dogs, hunting dogs, companion dogs, etc.

A parent club is the national organization, sanctioned by the AKC, which promotes and safeguards its breed in the country. The Standard Schnauzer Club of America was formed in 1933 and can be found online at www.standardschnauzer.org. The parent club holds an annual national specialty show, usually in a different city each year, in which many of the country's top dogs, handlers and breeders gather to compete. At a specialty show, only members of a single breed are invited to participate. There are also group specialties, in which all members of a group are invited. For more information about dog clubs in your area, contact the AKC at www.akc.org on the Internet or write them at their Raleigh, NC address.

HOW SHOWS ARE ORGANIZED

Three kinds of conformation shows are offered by the AKC. There is the all-breed show, in which all AKC-recognized breeds can compete; the specialty show, which is for one breed only and usually sponsored by the breed's parent club and the group show, for all breeds in one of the AKC's seven groups. The Standard Schnauzer competes in the Working Group.

For a dog to become an AKC champion of record, the dog must earn 15 points at shows. The points must be awarded by at least three different judges and must include two "majors" under different judges. A "major" is a three-, four- or five-point win, and the number of points per win is determined by the number of dogs competing in the show on that day. (Dogs that are absent or are excused are not counted.) The number of points that are awarded varies from breed to breed. More dogs are needed to attain a major in more popular breeds, and fewer dogs are needed in less popular breeds. Yearly, the AKC evaluates the number of dogs in competition in each division (there are 14 divisions in all, based on geography) and may or may not change the numbers of dogs required for each number of points. For example, a major in Division 2 (Delaware, New Jersey and Pennsylvania) recently required 17 dogs or 16 bitches for a three-point major, 29 dogs or 27 bitches for a four-point major and 51 dogs or 46 bitches for a five-point major. The Standard Schnauzer attracts numerically proportionate representation at all-breed shows.

A Group win for Am./Can. Ch. Von Stocker's The Jig Is Up, "Jiggs," owned and bred by Lucille Warren, co-owned by Dean Gehnert and Lucy Bitz.

Only one dog and one bitch of each breed can win points at a given show. There are no "co-ed" classes except for champions of record. Dogs and bitches do not compete against each other until they are champions. Dogs that are not champions (referred to as "class dogs") compete in one of five classes. The class in which a dog is entered depends on age and previous show wins. First there is the Puppy Class (sometimes divided further into classes for 6- to 9-month-olds and 9- to 12-month-olds); next is the Novice Class (for dogs that have no points toward their championships and whose only first-place wins have come in the Puppy Class or the Novice Class, the latter class limited to three first

places); then there is the American-bred Class (for dogs bred in the US); the Bred-by-Exhibitor Class (for dogs handled by their breeders or by immediate family members of their breeders) and the Open Class (for any non-champions). Any dog may enter the Open Class, regardless of age or win history, but to be competitive the dog should be older and have ring experience.

The judge at the show begins judging the male dogs in the Puppy Class(es) and proceeds through the other classes. The judge awards first through fourth place in each class. The first-place winners of each class then compete with one another in the Winners Class to determine Winners Dog. The judge then starts over with the bitches, beginning with the Puppy Class(es) and proceeding up to the Winners Class to award Winners Bitch, just as he did with the dogs. A Reserve Winners Dog and Reserve Winners Bitch are also selected; they could be awarded the points in the case of a disqualification.

The Winners Dog and Winners Bitch are the two that are awarded the points for their breed. They then go on to compete with any champions of record (often called "specials") of their breed that are entered in the show. The champions may be dogs or bitches; in this class, all are shown together. The judge reviews the Winners Dog and Winners Bitch along with all of the champions to select the Best of

Winning Best of Breed is Ch. Stahlkreiger Lanni v. Nirvana, "Lanni," with owner Cheryl Crompton.

Breed winner. The Best of Winners is selected between the Winners Dog and Winners Bitch; if one of these two is selected Best of Breed as well, he or she is automatically determined Best of Winners. Lastly, the judge selects Best of Opposite Sex to the Best of Breed winner. The Best of Breed winner then goes on to the group competition.

At a group or all-breed show, the Best of Breed winners from each breed are divided into their respective groups to compete against one another for Group One through Group Four. Group One is awarded to the dog that best lives up to the ideal for his breed as described in the standard. A group judge, therefore, must have a thorough working knowledge of many breed standards. After placements have been made in each group, the seven Group One winners (from the Working Group, Toy Group, Hound Group, etc.) compete against each other for the top honor, Best in Show.

There are different ways to find out about dog shows in your area. The American Kennel Club's monthly magazine, the *American Kennel Gazette,* is accompanied by the *Events Calendar;* this magazine is available through subscription. You can also look on the AKC's and your parent club's websites for information and check the event listings in your local newspaper.

Your Standard Schnauzer must be six months of age or older and

Ch. Charisma Jackie-O, showing off the breed's powerful and impressive gait.

registered with the AKC in order to be entered in AKC-sanctioned shows in which there are classes for the Standard Schnauzer. Your Standard Schnauzer also must not possess any disqualifying faults and must be sexually intact. The reason for the latter is simple: dog shows are the proving grounds to determine which dogs and bitches are worthy of being bred. If they cannot be bred, that defeats the purpose! On that note, only dogs that have achieved championships, thus proving their excellent quality, should be bred. If you have spayed or neutered your dog, however, there are many AKC events other than conformation, such as obedience trials, agility trials and the Canine Good Citizen® Program, in which you and your Standard Schnauzer can participate.

Argenta's Emmett from Sweden, proudly displaying his curly tail. Sweden forbids tail docking and ear cropping.

OTHER TYPES OF COMPETITION

In addition to conformation shows, the AKC holds a variety of other competitive events. Obedience trials, agility trials and tracking trials are open to all breeds, while hunting tests, field trials, lure coursing, herding tests and trials, earthdog tests and coonhound events are limited to specific breeds or groups of breeds. The Junior

Ch. Pepper Tree You're My Girl, winning an Award of Merit at an SSCA national specialty, with her owner Arden Holst.

Showmanship program is offered to aspiring young handlers and their dogs, and the Canine Good Citizen® Program is an all-around good-behavior test open to all dogs, pure-bred and mixed.

OBEDIENCE TRIALS

Mrs. Helen Whitehouse Walker, a Standard Poodle fancier, can be credited with introducing obedience trials to the United States. In the 1930s she designed a series of exercises based on those of the Associated Sheep, Police, Army Dog Society of Great Britain. These exercises were intended to evaluate the working relationship between dog and owner. Since those early days of the sport in the US, obedience trials have grown more and more popular, and now more than 2,000 trials each year attract over 100,000 dogs and their owners. Any dog registered with the AKC, regardless of neutering or other disqualifications that would preclude entry in conformation competition, can participate in obedience trials.

There are three levels of difficulty in obedience competition. The first (and easiest) level is the Novice, in which dogs can earn the Companion Dog (CD) title. The intermediate level is the Open level, in which the Companion Dog Excellent (CDX) title is awarded. The advanced level is the Utility level, in which dogs compete for the Utility Dog (UD) title. Classes at each level are further divided into "A" and "B," with "A" for beginners and "B" for those with more experience. In order to win a title at a given level, a dog must earn three "legs." A "leg" is accomplished when a dog scores 170 or higher (200 is a perfect score). The scoring system gets a little trickier when you understand that a dog must score more than 50% of the points available for each exercise in order to actually earn the points. Available points for each exercise range between 20 and 40.

Once he's earned the UD title, a

Am./Can. Ch. Oakwood Applejack UD, known as "Conrad," with owner Anne Miller after a successful day in obedience. The UD (Utility Dog) title is prestigious and difficult to earn.

dog can go on to win the prestigious title of Utility Dog Excellent (UDX) by winning "legs" in ten shows. Additionally, Utility Dogs who win "legs" in Open B and Utility B earn points toward the lofty title of Obedience Trial Champion (OTCh.). Established in 1977 by the AKC, this title requires a dog to earn 100 points as well as three first places in a combination of Open B and Utility B classes

Some dog clubs offer practice facilities to prepare dogs for events like obedience and agility.

MEET THE AKC

The American Kennel Club is the main governing body of the dog sport in the United States. Founded in 1884, the AKC consists of 500 or more independent dog clubs plus 4,500 affiliated clubs, all of which follow the AKC rules and regulations. Additionally, the AKC maintains a registry for pure-bred dogs in the US and works to preserve the integrity of the sport and its continuation in the country. Over 1,000,000 dogs are registered each year, representing about 150 recognized breeds. There are over 15,000 competitive events held annually for which over 2,000,000 dogs enter to participate. Dogs compete to earn over 40 different titles, from champion to Companion Dog to Master Agility Champion.

under three different judges. The "brass ring" of obedience competition is the AKC's National Obedience Invitational. This is an exclusive competition for only the cream of the obedience crop. In order to qualify for the invitational, a dog must be ranked in either the top 25 all-breeds in obedience or in the top three for his breed in obedience. The title at stake here is that of National Obedience Champion (NOC).

AGILITY TRIALS

Agility trials became sanctioned by the AKC in August 1994, when the first licensed agility trials were held. Since that time, agility certainly has grown in popularity by leaps and bounds, literally! The AKC allows all registered breeds (including Miscellaneous Class breeds) to participate, providing the dog is 12 months of age or older. Agility is designed so that the handler demonstrates how well the dog can

work at his side. The handler directs his dog through, over, under and around an obstacle course that includes jumps, tires, the dog walk, weave poles, pipe tunnels, collapsed tunnels and more. While working his way through the course, the dog must keep one eye and ear on the handler and the rest of his body on the course. The handler runs along with the dog, giving verbal and hand signals to guide the dog through the course.

The first organization to promote agility trials in the US was the United States Dog Agility Association, Inc. (USDAA). Established in 1986, the USDAA sparked the formation of many member clubs around the country. To participate in USDAA trials, dogs must be at least 18 months of age. The USDAA and AKC both offer titles to winning dogs, although the exercises and requirements of the two organizations differ.

Agility trials are a great way to keep your dog active, and they will keep you running, too! You should join a local agility club to learn more about the sport. These clubs offer sessions in which you can introduce your dog to the various obstacles as well as training classes to prepare him for competition. In no time, your dog will be climbing A-frames, crossing the dog walk and flying over hurdles, all with you right beside him. Your heart will leap every time your dog jumps through the hoop.

The obedience broad jump looks easy when watching a Standard Schnauzer in action.

The TD level is the first and most basic level in tracking, progressing in difficulty to the TDX and then the VST. A dog must follow a track laid by a human 30 to 120 minutes prior in order to earn the TD title. The track is about 500 yards long and contains up to 5 directional changes. At the next level, the TDX, the dog must follow a 3- to 5-hour-old track over a course that is up to 1,000 yards long and has up to 7 directional changes. In the most difficult level, the VST, the track is up to 5 hours old and located in an urban setting.

This agility exercise includes jumping over a hurdle with a removable top bar. Some Standard Schnauzers are superior jumpers and take to this exercise with exceptional grace.

TRACKING

Tracking tests are exciting ways to test your Standard Schnauzer's instinctive scenting ability on a competitive level. All dogs have a nose, and all breeds are welcome in tracking tests. The first AKC-licensed tracking test took place in 1937 as part of the Utility level at an obedience trial, and thus competitive tracking was officially begun. The first title, Tracking Dog (TD), was offered in 1947, ten years after the first official tracking test. It was not until 1980 that the AKC added the title Tracking Dog Excellent (TDX), which was followed by the title Variable Surface Tracking (VST) in 1995. Champion Tracker (CT) is awarded to a dog who has earned all three of those titles.

HERDING EVENTS

The Standard Schnauzer has been recognized as having been used as a herding and droving dog from early in its history. All early references to the breed refer to it as an all-purpose farm dog and drover. In *Hutchinson's Dog Encyclopaedia* (circa 1935), it states: "The Schnauzer is a herd dog, and is

A tracking lesson on a cold morning. Is there anything that this breed cannot do?

Geistvoll Crème de la Crème, Hannah, herding at high speed. Herding is an exciting area in which more and more Standard Schnauzers and their owners are getting involved.

largely used as a cattle and drover's dog, owing to its extreme agility. The Schnauzer is in no way related to the Terrier group, but belongs to the Shepherd-dog group."

Back in the 1990s Standard Schnauzer owners in California found that generations of city and suburban life had not dimmed the breed's instincts to herd. Herding events (either informal or sanctioned by the American Herding Breeds Association [AHBA]) have been held since 1999 at the Standard Schnauzer Club of America's (SSCA) national specialty. A prominent AKC and AHBA judge once said that he felt that the Standard Schnauzer was the best-kept secret in the herding world. Another judge also commented that there is more herding desire and ability in the Standard Schnauzer

than in some of the more traditionally known herding breeds.

Herding has become a popular activity for Standard Schnauzers and their owners throughout the United States in recent years. The breed has exhibited a very high (around 85%) pass rate at both informal and AHBA-sanctioned instinct tests. The SSCA actively worked to have the breed approved to participate in AKC herding tests and trials, and in 2004 their efforts paid off, as Standard Schnauzers are now eligible to participate in AKC herding events. The SSCA hopes that in the very near future the Standard Schnauzer will be an important breed at herding trials and that owners of this very talented breed will keep adding titles on their dogs.

Herding events are designed to evaluate the dogs' herding instincts, and the aim is to develop these innate skills and show that herding dogs today can still perform the functions for which they were originally intended, whether or not they are actually used in working capacities. Herding events are designed to simulate farm situations and are held on two levels: tests and trials.

AKC herding tests are more basic and are scored on a pass/fail system, meaning that dogs do not compete against each other to earn titles. Titles at this level are Herding Tested (HT) and the more difficult Pre-Trial Tested (PT). In addition, there is a non-competitive certification program, Herding Instinct Tested, which gives you a chance to evaluate the potential that your dog may have for herding. If your dog successfully passes this test, he receives a Herding Instinct Certificate, which makes him eligible to enter herding trials.

The more challenging herding trial level is competitive and requires more training and experience. There are three different courses (A, B and C, each with a different type of farm situation) with different types of livestock (cattle, sheep or ducks). There are three titles available on each course, Herding Started, Herding Intermediate and Herding Advanced, with each level being progressively more difficult. Handlers can choose the type of course and type of livestock for their dogs based on the breed's typical use. Once a Herding Advanced title has been earned on a course, the dog can then begin to strive for the Herding Champion title.

Other specialty organizations hold trials that are open to all herding breeds; the way these events are structured and the titles that are awarded differ from those of the AKC. For example, the AHBA allows any breed with herding in its ancestry to participate, as well as allowing mixed-breed herding dogs. To pass the Herding Instinct Test, the handler works with the dog at the shepherd's direction while the

shepherd evaluates the dog's willingness to approach, move and round up the sheep while at the same time following the instructions of his handler.

At the competition level in AHBA events, dogs work with their handlers to move sheep up and down the field, through gates and into a pen, and also to hold the sheep without a pen, all while being timed. This is an amazing sight to see! A good dog working with the shepherd has to be the ultimate man-dog interaction. Rare breeds were often traditionally used for herding and, fortunately, the AHBA is more than happy to have rare breeds participate. Club members and spectators love to welcome some of these wonderful dogs that they have only read about but never seen.

Hannah has rounded up the sheep and leads them into the pen.

STANDARD SCHNAUZER

You chose your dog because something clicked the minute you set eyes on him. Or perhaps it seemed that the dog selected you and that's what clinched the deal. Either way, you are now investing time and money in this dog, a true pal and an outstanding member of the family. Everything about him is perfect…well, almost perfect. Remember, he is a dog! For that matter, how does he think *you're* doing?

AGGRESSION

Aggression is a problem that concerns all responsible dog owners. Aggression can be a very big and serious problem in dogs and, when not controlled, it always becomes dangerous. Most aggression is due to the dog's thinking that he holds the number-one spot in the family pack, and it is a sign of dominance. Aggression also can be caused by fear.

The very first time you see your Standard Schnauzer puppy showing any signs of aggression, whether caused by fear or dominance, contact a trainer, preferably a behaviorist that has a working knowledge of the breed. An experienced behaviorist can tell by the dog's body language if the dog's aggression stems from dominance or fear, as aggression must be dealt with in different ways with different methods depending on the cause. When this type of behavior is nipped in the bud and handled properly at a young age, you can mold the dog's reactions into acceptable ones.

Regarding dominant aggression, dogs instinctively know that there must be a leader. If you are not the obvious choice for king, your dog will assume the throne! These conflicting innate desires of wanting to please his owner but being ready to become top dog are what owners are up against when setting out in training. Some dogs, just like some people, have a bigger

When you build a bond of affection and trust with your dog from an early age, he will be more responsive to you as his leader.

sense of self-worth and very strong innate desires for leadership.

An important part of training is taking every opportunity to reinforce that you are the leader. One of the simplest ways to assert leadership with your dog is to use food. The leader provides the food for the pack. Never give the dog his

What a bond! The affection is obvious between Am./Can. Ch. Oakwood Carolina Belle, known as "Vicki," and her owner Anne Miler.

THE MACHO DOG

The Venus/Mars differences are found in dogs, too. Males have distinct behaviors that, while seemingly sex-related, are more closely connected to the role of the male as leader. Marking territory by urinating on it is one means that male dogs use to establish their presence. Doing so merely says, "I've been here." Small dogs often attempt to lift their legs higher on the tree than the previous male. While this is natural behavior outdoors on items like telephone poles, fence posts, fire hydrants and most other upright objects, marking indoors is totally unacceptable. Treat it as you would a house-training accident and clean thoroughly to eradicate the scent. Another behavior often seen in the macho male, mounting is a dominance display. Neutering the dog before six months of age helps to deter this behavior. You can discourage him from mounting by catching the dog as he's about to mount you, stepping quickly aside and saying "Off!"

food without first making him do something. It can be as simple as making the dog sit and wait while you put his food bowl down. Also, never give in to your dog's pleading eyes and wagging tail for an extra treat unless he first does something that you want him to do.

As a rule of thumb, positive reinforcement is what works best. With a dominant dog, punishment and negative reinforcement can have the opposite effect of what

At the Fisher household, a friendly sparring match between Igor and his feline companion Spode is a daily event.

With body language that could be mistaken for aggression, these friends are actually enjoying an invigorating play session.

Dog-to-dog introductions should be done under supervision and on loose leads. A tightly pulled lead can make a dog tense and agitated when meeting another dog.

you want to accomplish. Remember that a dominant dog perceives himself at the top of the social ladder, and he will fight to keep that status quo. The best way to prevent this from happening is to never give him reason to think that he is in control in the first place. Find a good trainer or behavior specialist, one who does not use or rely on harsh methods. Scolding is necessary now and then, but the focus with a dominant dog in training should always be on positive reinforcement.

Do not think that you can handle aggression alone, because once the dog is an adult, it is almost impossible to eradicate the problem totally. By this time he will be in the habit of acting aggressively and may even have become a biter. An aggressive dog is unpredictable; you never know when he going to strike or what he is going to do. An aggressive dog cannot be trusted, and a dog that cannot be trusted is not safe to have as a family pet. You cannot rehome an aggressive dog unless you know what is causing the aggression and you know that rehoming him will eliminate this cause; further, the new owners must be knowledgeable about and fully aware of the

issues and must understand how to handle the dog. In some cases, unfortunately, aggressive dogs have to be euthanized.

Another type of aggression, that which is directed toward other dogs, usually is fear-based but sometimes can be dominance-based. Either type can be eliminated or controlled through very early socialization with other puppies and dogs.

Dogs, like people, have their own "personal space." Also like people, some dogs have a larger personal space than others. If you find that other dogs make your Standard Schnauzer very nervous or agitated, redirect his attention back to you, with a very tasty morsel in your hand, and remove him from the situation. Proper praise for good behavior is essential with a dog like this. The best way to deal with dog-aggression is to find a reputable trainer to work with you to overcome this problem as quickly as possible.

A milder form of aggression is the dog's guarding anything that he perceives to be his—his food dish, his toys, his bed and/or his crate. This can be prevented if you take firm control from the start. The young puppy can and should be taught that his leader will share, but that certain rules apply. Guarding is mild aggression only in the beginning stages, and it will worsen and become dangerous if you let it.

> ## DOMINANCE
> Dogs are born with dominance skills, meaning that they can be quite clever in trying to get their way. The "follow-me" trot to the cookie jar is an example. The toy dropped in your lap says "Play with me." The leash delivered to you along with an excited look means "Take me for a walk." These are all good-natured dominant behaviors. Ask your dog to sit before agreeing to his request and you'll remain "top dog."

When dealing with guarding behavior, don't try to snatch anything away from your puppy. Bargain for the item in question so that you can positively reinforce him when he gives it up. Punishment only results in worsening any aggressive behavior.

Many dogs extend their guarding impulse toward items they've stolen. The dog figures, "If I have it, it's mine!" (Some ill-behaved kids have similar tendencies.) An angry confrontation will only increase the dog's aggression. (Have you ever watched a child have a tantrum?) Also remember that direct eye contact can be threatening to some dogs. Try a simple distraction first, such as tossing a toy or picking up his leash for a walk. If that doesn't work, the best way to handle the situation is with basic obedience. Show the dog a treat, followed by

It's normal for your Standard Schnauzer to anticipate your return, but it becomes a problem if he pines for you all day.

calm, almost slow-motion commands: "Come. Sit. Drop it. Good dog," and then hand over the cheese! That's one example of positive-reinforcement training.

Children can be bitten when they try to retrieve a stolen shoe or toy, so they need to know how to handle the dog or to let an adult do it. They may also be bitten as they run away from a dog, in either fear or play. The dog sees the child's running as reason for pursuit, and even a friendly young puppy will nip at the heels of a runaway. Teach the kids not to run away from a strange dog and when to stop overly exciting play with their own puppy.

Fear biting is yet another aggressive behavior. A fear biter gives many warning signals. The dog leans away from the approaching person (sometimes hiding behind his owner) with his ears and tail down, but not in submission. He may even shiver. His hackles are raised, his lips curled. When the person steps into the dog's "flight zone" (a circle of 1 to 3 feet surrounding the dog), he attacks. Because of the fear factor, he performs a rapid attack-and-retreat. Because it is directed at a person, vets are often the victims of this form of aggression. It is frightening, but discovering and eliminating the cause of the fright will help overcome the dog's need to bite. Early socialization plays a strong role in the prevention of this

behavior. Again, if you can't cope with it, get the help of an expert.

SEPARATION ANXIETY
Most dogs do not like for the "family pack" to leave them. In the wild the pack usually stays together, but in the wild the pack leader does not have to keep appointments or report for work. Any behaviorist will tell you that separation anxiety is the most common problem about which pet owners complain. It is also one of the easiest to prevent. A dog that

whimpers to indicate his displeasure as you are leaving him is normal. Separation anxiety, however, is much more serious and can lead to destructive behavior. Unfortunately, a behaviorist usually is not consulted until the dog is a stressed-out, neurotic mess. At that stage, it is indeed a problem that requires the help of a professional.

Training the puppy to the fact that people in the house come and go is essential in order to avoid this anxiety. Leaving the puppy in his crate or a confined area while family members go in and out, and stay out for longer and longer periods of time, is the basic way to desensitize the pup to the family's frequent departures. If you are at home most of every day, make it a point to go out for at least an hour or two whenever possible.

How you leave is vital to the dog's reaction. Your dog is no fool. He knows the difference between sweats and business suits, jeans and dresses. He sees you pat your pocket to check for your wallet, open your briefcase, check that you have your cell phone or pick up the car keys. He knows from the hurry of the kids in the morning that they're off to school until afternoon. Lipstick? Aftershave lotion? Lunch boxes? Every move you make registers in his sensory perception and memory. Your puppy knows more about your departures than you do. You can't get away with a thing!

Before you got dressed, you checked the dog's water bowl and his supply of long-lasting chew toys, and you turned the radio on low. You will leave him in his "safe" area, not with total freedom of the house. If you've invested in child safety gates, you can be reasonably sure that he'll remain in the designated area. Don't give him access to a window where he can watch you leave the house. If you're leaving for an hour or two, just put him into his crate with a safe toy.

Now comes the test! You are ready to walk out the door. Do not give your Standard Schnauzer a big hug and a fond farewell. Do not drag out a long goodbye. Those are the very things that jump-start separation anxiety. Toss a biscuit into the dog's area, call out "So long, pooch" and close the door. You're gone. The chances are that the dog may bark a couple of times, or maybe whine once or twice, and then settle down to enjoy his biscuit and take a lovely nap, especially if you took him for a nice long walk before you left. As he grows up, the barks and whines will stop because it's an old routine, so why should he make the effort?

When you first brought home the puppy, the come-and-go routine was intermittent and constant. He was put into his crate with a tiny treat. You left (silently) and returned in 3 minutes, then 5, then

You might be surprised by your pup's choice of chew-worthy items, but nothing is off limits in the eyes of a teething pup.

10, then 15, then half an hour, until finally you could leave without a problem and be gone for 2 or 3 hours. If, at any time in the future, there's a "separation" problem, refresh his memory by going back to that basic training.

Now comes the next most important part—your return. Do not make a big production of coming home. "Hi, poochie" is as grand a greeting as he needs. When you've taken off your hat and coat, tossed your briefcase on the hall table and glanced at the mail, and the dog has settled down from the

excitement of seeing you "in person" from his confined area, then go and give him a warm, friendly greeting. A potty trip is needed and a walk would be appreciated, since he's been such a good dog.

CHEWING

All puppies chew. All dogs chew. This is a fact of life for canines, and sometimes you may think it's what your dog does best! A pup starts chewing when his first set of teeth erupts and continues throughout the teething period. Chewing gives the pup relief from itchy gums and incoming teeth and, from that time on, he gets great satisfaction out of this normal, somewhat idle, canine activity. Providing safe chew toys is the best way to direct this behavior in an appropriate manner. Chew toys are available in all sizes, textures and flavors, but you must monitor the wear-and-tear inflicted on your pup's toys to be sure that the ones you've chosen are safe and remain in good condition.

Dogs cannot distinguish between a rawhide toy and a nice leather shoe or wallet. It's up to you to keep your possessions away from the dog and to keep your eye on the dog. There's a form of destruction caused by chewing that is not the dog's fault. Let's say you allow him on the sofa. One day he takes a rawhide bone up on the sofa and, in the course of chewing on the bone, takes up a bit of fabric.

Stuffed toys are favorites of Standard Schnauzers, although they probably won't stay stuffed for long.

He continues to chew. Disaster! Now you've learned the lesson: dogs with chew toys have to be either kept off furniture and carpets, carefully supervised or put into their confined areas for chew time.

DIGGING

Digging, which is seen as a destructive behavior to humans, is another natural and normal doggy behavior. For some Standard Schnauzers, digging is a way of life and is most frustrating to their owners. Digging is a normal thing for the wild dog when finding food and making shelter. Your Standard Schnauzer has no reason to do this, as you provide him with food and shelter. So, if your Standard Schnauzer is digging in your yard or garden, he may be attempting to exterminate some wee critter that's been poking around in your petunias. Remember that the breed's traditional uses include ratting and other vermin control.

Domesticated dogs also dig to escape, and that's a lot more dangerous than it is destructive. A dog that digs under the fence is the one that is hit by a car or becomes lost. A good fence to protect a digger should be set 10 to 12 inches below ground level, and every fence needs to be routinely checked for even the smallest openings that can become possible escape routes.

Catching your dog in the act of

THE ROSY SIDE OF DIGGING

Digging is one of those problems that must be caught and dealt with early on. Unless you can actually catch the pup in the act, you cannot scold him at all. There is an interesting method, though, that puts a positive spin on an unwanted behavior. When you find a puppy crater in your flower garden, take one of the pup's feces, put it in the hole and cover it up with dirt. This serves the purpose of getting rid of something you do not want in your yard, and your flowers will prosper. It might take a week or two, but it does work. I knew one kennel owner that had the most beautiful rose garden—thanks to her dogs!

---

digging is the easiest way to stop it, because your dog will make the "one-plus-one" connection, but digging is too often a solitary occupation, something the lonely dog does out of boredom. Catch your young puppy in the act and put a stop to it before you have a yard full of craters. It is more difficult to stop if your dog sees you gardening. If you can dig, why can't he? Because you say so, that's why! Some dogs are excavation experts, and some dogs are less inclined. When it comes to any of these instinctive canine behaviors, we can never say "never."

BARKING

Standard Schnauzers are not extremely noisy dogs, nor are they dogs that bark just for the heck of it, although I did at one time own a Standard Schnauzer that always gave out two distinctive "woofs" when she first went out into the yard, and then would turn and give two more very distinctive "woofs" just as she was about to go back into the house. I always thought of her as saying, "I'm here, world!" and "See you later, world!"

Fortunately, Standard Schnauzers tend to use their barks purposefully. The Standard Schnauzer will always set off an alarm bark when he hears a strange sound. Some will bark a happy bark when they hear their owners arriving home. But woe is to the stranger that does not heed their deep warning bark.

The Standard Schnauzer is an excellent and discerning family watchdog but occasionally, if not instructed otherwise, he can get carried away with himself when

> **DOGS OF PREY**
> Chasing small animals is in the blood of many dogs, perhaps most; they think that this is a fun recreational activity (although some are more likely to bring you an undesirable "gift" as a result of the hunt). The good old "Leave it" command works to deter your dog from taking off in pursuit of "prey," but only if taught with the dog on leash for control. The same principle applies for a dog who chases cars or bikes.

guests arrive. I have found that a quiet "Thank you" (for the watchdog work), followed by "That's enough now," meaning "Quiet so I can greet my guests," works very well. I am a firm believer in praising dogs for a job well done.

FOOD-RELATED PROBLEMS
We're not talking about eating, diets or nutrition here, we're talking about bad habits. Face it. All dogs are beggars. Food is the motivation for everything we want our dogs to do and, when you combine that with their innate ability to "con" us in order to get their way, it's a wonder there aren't far more obese dogs in the world.

Who can resist the bleeding-heart look that says "I'm starving," or the paw that gently pats your knee and gives you a knowing

"Share and share alike" is the message that this pup is trying to convey to his young friend.

look, or the whining "please" or even the total body language of a perfect sit beneath the cookie jar. No one who professes to love his dog can turn down the pleas of his clever canine's performances every time. One thing is for sure, though: definitely do not allow begging at the table. Family meals do not include your dog.

Control your dog's begging habit by making your dog work for his rewards. Ignore his begging when you can. Utilize the obedience commands you've taught your dog. Use "Off" for the pawing. A sit or even a long down will interrupt the whining. His reward in these situations is definitely not a treat! Casual verbal praise is enough. Be sure all members of the family follow the same rules. There is a different type of begging that does demand your immediate response and that is the appeal to be let (or taken) outside! Usually that is a quick paw or small whine to get your attention, followed by a race to the door. This type of begging needs your quick attention and approval. Of course, a really smart dog will soon figure out how to cut you off at the pass and direct you to that cookie jar on your way to the door! Some dogs are always one step ahead of us.

Stealing food is a problem only if you are not paying attention. A dog can't steal food out of his reach. Leaving your dog

Some Standard Schnauzers will go to any lengths to steal a morsel from your countertop. It's best to keep food out of the reach of your "always famished" dog!

in the kitchen with the roast beef on the table is asking for trouble. Putting cheese and crackers on the coffee table also requires a watchful eye to stop the would-be thief in his tracks. The word to use (one word, remember, even if it's two words pronounced as one) is "Leave it!" Instead of preceding it with yet another "No," try using a guttural sound like "Aagh!" That sounds more like a warning growl to the dog and therefore has instant meaning.

Canine thieves are in their element when little kids are carrying cookies in their hands! Your dog will think he's been exceptionally clever if he causes a child to drop a cookie. Bonanza! The easiest solution is to keep dog and children separated at snack time. You must also be sure that the children understand that they must not tease the dog with food—his or theirs. Your dog does not mean to bite the kids, but when he snatches at a tidbit so near the level of his mouth, it can result in an unintended nip.

My Standard Schnauzer

PUT YOUI

Dog's Name _____

Date _____ Photographer _____